A CAT Book

A CAT Book

PaRragon

Bath · New York · Singapore · Hong Kong · Cologne · Delhi · Melbourne

This is a Parragon Publishing Book
This edition published in 2007

Parragon Publishing
Queen Street House
4 Queen Street
Bath BA1 1HE, UK

Designers: Timothy Shaner and Christopher Measom
Project Director: Alice Wong
Project Assistants: Kate DeWitt and Jeffrey McCord
Cat Tales retold by Deidra Garcia
Living with Cats, Cat Training, Fun and Games, and Kitty Treats text by Ellen Leach

Printed in Thailand.

Contents

Poetry

Training and Tricks

Fun and Games

Contents

Kitty Treats

If man could be crossed
with the cat, it would
improve man, but
deteriorate the cat.

— MARK TWAIN

Adopting a Cat

Think seriously about whether your lifestyle and budget can accommodate a pet. Cats are creatures of routine and require a stable living environment, regular care, and affection. If you've never owned a cat before, be sure to pick up a book or pamphlet on their care. Make sure you can afford the kind of monetary and emotional commitment it takes to become a companion to a furry child who can live to be 15 or even 20 years old.

There are organizations, including the American Society for the Protection of Animals (ASPCA), Humane Society, Bide-A-Wee, and local pet rescue groups, that will defray the costs of spaying, neutering, and vaccinations. In addition, these organizations often run clinics that provide discounted vet care. Consider adopting an abandoned animal from a shelter.

If you have your heart set on a purebred, be sure to contact a reputable breeder with checkable references and certification through the Cat Fanciers' Association (CFA) or the International Cat Association (TICA). In addition to the cute kittens you see at the cattery, consider adopting a full-grown cat who is being "retired." These often young show-quality adults have done their stints in the breeding and show circuits, and make terrific pets. An older cat can be a kinder, gentler companion.

The Cat's Paradise
by Emile Zola

I was then two years old, and was at the same time the fattest and most naive cat in existence. At that tender age I still had all the presumptuousness of an animal who is disdainful of the sweetness of home.

How fortunate I was, indeed, that providence had placed me with your aunt! That good woman adored me. I had at the bottom of a wardrobe a veritable sleeping salon, with feather cushions and triple covers. My food was equally excellent; never just bread, or soup, but always meat, carefully chosen meat.

Well, in the midst of all this opulence, I had only one desire, one dream, and that was to slip out of the upper window and escape on to the roofs. Caresses annoyed me, the softness of my bed nauseated me, and I was so fat that it was disgusting even to myself. In short, I was bored the whole day long just with being happy.

I must tell you that by stretching my neck a bit, I had seen the roof directly in front of my window. That day four cats were playing with each other up there; their fur bristling, their tails high, they were romping around with every indication of joy on the blue roof slates baked by the sun. I had never before watched such an extraordinary spectacle. And from then on I had a definitely fixed belief: out there on that roof was true happiness, out there beyond the window which was always closed so carefully. In proof of that contention I remembered that the doors of the chest in which the meat was kept were also closed, just as carefully!

I resolved to flee. After all

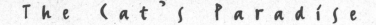

there had to be other things in life besides a comfortable bed. Out there was the unknown, the ideal. And then one day they forgot to close the kitchen window. I jumped out on to the small roof above it.

How beautiful the roofs were! The wide eaves bordering them exuded delicious smells. Carefully I followed those eaves, where my feet sank into the fine mud that smelled tepid and infinitely sweet. It felt as if I were walking on velvet. And the sun shone with a good warmth that caressed my plumpness.

I will not hide from you the fact that I was trembling all over. There was something overwhelming in my joy. I remember particularly the tremendous emotional upheaval which actually made me lose my footing on the slates, when three cats rolled down from the ridge of the roof and approached with excited miaows. But when I showed signs of fear, they told me I was a silly fat goose and insisted that their miaowing was only laughter.

I decided to join them in their cater-wauling. It was fun, even though the three stalwarts weren't as fat as I was and made fun of me when I rolled like a ball over the roof heated by the sun.

An old tomcat belonging to the gang honored me particularly with his friendship. He offered to take care of my education, an offer which I accepted with gratitude.

Oh, how far away seemed all the soft things of your aunt! I drank from the gutters, and never did sugared milk taste half as fine! Everything was good and beautiful.

A female cat passed by, a ravishing she, and the very sight of her filled me with strange emotions. Only in my dreams had I up to then seen such an exquisite creature with such a magnificently arched back. We dashed forward to meet the newcomer, my three companions

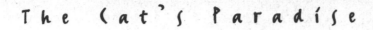

and myself. I was actually ahead of the others in paying the enchanting female my compliments; but then one of my comrades gave me a nasty bite in the neck, and I let out a shriek of pain.

"Pshaw!" said the old tomcat, dragging me away. "You will meet plenty of others."

After a walk that lasted an hour I had a ravenous appetite.

"What does one eat on these roofs?" I asked my friend the tom.

"Whatever one finds," he replied laconically.

This answer embarrassed me somewhat for, hunt as I might, I couldn't find a thing. Finally I looked through a dormer window and saw a young workman preparing his breakfast. On the table, just above the windowsill, lay a

chop of a particularly succulent red.

"There is my chance," I thought, rather naively.

So I jumped on to the table and snatched the chop. But the working-

man saw me and gave me a terrific wallop across my back with a broom. I dropped the meat, cursed rather vulgarly and escaped.

"What part of the world do you come from?" asked the tom-

The Cat's Paradise

cat. "Don't you know that meat on tables is meant only to be admired from afar? What we've got to do is look in the gutters."

I have never been able to understand why kitchen meat shouldn't belong to cats. My stomach began to complain quite bitterly. The tom tried to console me by saying it would only be necessary to wait for the night. Then, he said, we would climb down from the roofs into the streets and forage in the garbage heaps.

Wait for the night! Confirmed philosopher that he was, he said it calmly while the very thought of such a protracted fast made me positively faint.

Night came ever so slowly, a misty night that made me shiver. To make things worse, rain began to fall, a thin, penetrating rain whipped up by brisk howling gusts of wind.

How desolate the streets looked to me! There was noth-

ing left of the good warmth, of the big sun, of those roofs where one could play so pleasantly. My paws slipped on the slimy pavement, and I began to think with some longing of my triple covers and my feather pillow.

We had hardly reached the street when my friend, the tom, began to tremble. He made himself small, quite small, and glided surreptitiously along the walls of the houses, warning me under his breath to be quick about it. When we reached the shelter of a house door, he hid behind it and purred with satisfaction. And when I asked him the reason for his strange conduct, he said:

"Did you see that man with the hook and the basket?"

"Yes."

"Well, if he had seen us, we would have been caught, fried on the spit and eaten!"

"Fried on the spit and eaten!" I exclaimed. "Why, then the

17

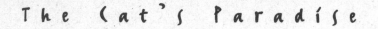

street is really not for the likes of us. One does not eat, but is eaten instead!"

In the meantime, however, they had begun to put the garbage out on the sidewalks. I inspected it with growing despair. All I found there were two or three dry bones that had obviously been thrown in among the ashes. And then and there I realized how succulent a dish of fresh meat really is!

My friend, the tom, went over the heaps of garbage with consummate artistry. He made me rummage around until morning, inspecting every cobblestone, without the least trace of hurry. But after ten hours of almost incessant rain my whole body was trembling. Damn the street, I thought, damn liberty! And how I longed for my prison!

When day came, the tomcat noticed that I was weakening.

"You've had enough, eh?" he asked in a strange voice.

"Oh, yes," I replied.

"Do you want to go home?"

"I certainly do. But how can I find my house?"

"Come along. Yesterday morning when I saw you come out I knew immediately that a cat as fat as you isn't made for the joys of liberty. I know where you live. I'll take you back to your door."

He said this all simply enough, the good, dignified tom. And when we finally got there, he added, without the slightest show of emotion:

"Goodbye, then."

"No, no!" I protested. "I shall not leave you like this. You come with me! We shall share bed and board. My mistress is a good woman . . ."

He didn't even let me finish.

"Shut up!" he said brusquely. "You are a fool. I'd die in that stuffy softness. Your abundant life is for weaklings. Free cats will never buy your comforts and your featherbeds at the price of being imprisoned. Goodbye!"

The Cat's Paradise

With these words he climbed back on to the roof. I saw his proud thin shadow shudder deliciously as it began to feel the warmth of the morning sun.

When I came home your aunt acted the martinet and administered a corrective which I received with profound joy. I reveled in being punished and voluptuously warm. And while she cuffed me, I thought with delight of the meat she would give me directly afterwards.

You see—an afterthought, while stretched out before the embers—true happiness, paradise, my master, is where one is locked up and beaten, wherever there is meat.

I speak for cats.

Hide-and-Seek for Treats

Ever wonder if you can teach your cat to come? Well, you can! All you need to do is teach her to associate her name with rewards, by treating consistently. Hide-and-Seek for Treats conditions the cat to come when alerted. (Think of it as "You've got food!" instead of "You've got mail!").

a human helper, one or more feline "hound dogs," a few of your cat's favorite (smelly) treats

1. Have your helper take the cat (or cats) into a closed room. (This alone will pique her interest; cats are always on the wrong side of a closed door.) Your assistant should count slowly to 100 while you hide in a closet, under a bed, or in another place. (Don't go up the ladder into the attic at first; increase the difficulty later.)

2. Release the cat.

3. Reward your cat with a treat as soon as she finds you. If she seems to give up, say pssst! or make some scratching sounds to teach her the game.

4. Repeat the above steps, choosing a new location. If you are behind a closet door, poke the treat out from under it when your cat locates you.

5. Once you've played a few rounds and your cat understands the game, add a cue. Rap the floor twice and say "Come!" as she is on her way to you. She will eventually associate this cue with you and the treats.

Feline Funnies

What's a cat's favorite dessert?
Chocolate mousse.

What happened to the cat who
swallowed a ball of yarn?
She had mittens.

What do cat actors say on stage?
Tabby or not tabby!

What did the cat say when
he lost all his money?
I'm paw.

What's the unluckiest kind
of cat to have?
A catastrophe!

Why did the cat join the Red Cross?
Because she wanted to be a first-aid kit.

What is the name of the unauthorized
autobiography of the cat?
Hiss and Tell.

Is it bad luck if a black cat follows you?
That depends on whether you're a man or a mouse.

If a cat is a flabby tabby, then
what is a very small cat?
An itty bitty kitty.

22

Dogs and Cats

by Pierre Loti

Cats are possessed of a shy, retiring nature, cajoling, haughty, and capricious, difficult to fathom. They reveal themselves only to certain favored individuals, and are repelled by the faintest suggestion of insult or even by the most trifling deception.

They are quite as intelligent as dogs, and are devoid of the yielding obsequiousness, the ridiculous sense of importance, and the revolting coarseness of these latter animals. Cats are dainty patricians, whereas dogs, whatever their social status, retain a *parvenu's* lack of cleanliness, and are irredeemably vulgar.

A cat is watching me. . . . He is close at hand, on the table, and thrusts forward his dimly thoughtful little head, into which some unwonted flash of intelligence has evidently just entered. Whilst servants or visitors have been on the spot, he has scornfully kept out of the way, under an armchair, for no other person than myself is allowed to stroke his invariably immaculate coat. But no sooner does he perceive that I am alone than he comes and sits in front of me, suddenly assuming one of those expressive looks that are seen from time to time in such enigmatical, contemplative

animals as belong to the same genus as himself. His yellow eyes look up at me, wide open, the pupils dilated by a mental effort to interrogate and attempt to understand: "Who are you, after all?" he asks. "Why do I trust you? Of what importance are you in the world? What are you thinking and doing here?"

In our ignorance of things, our inability to know anything, how amazing—perhaps terrifying—if we could but see into the curious depths of those eyes and fathom the *unknowable* within the little brain hidden away there! Ah! if only for a moment we could put ourselves in its place and afterwards remember, what an instantaneous and definite solution—though no doubt terrifying enough—we might obtain of the perplexing problems of life and eternity! Are these familiar animals our inferiors and far removed from us, or are they terribly near to us? Is the dark veil which conceals from them the cause and end of life more dense than that stretched before our own eyes? . . . No, never will it be our privilege to solve the secret of those little wheedling heads, which allow themselves so lovingly to be held and stroked, almost crushed, in our hands. . . .

And now he is about to sleep, maybe to dream, on this table at which I am writing; he settles down as close to me as possible, after stretching out his paw towards me two or three times, looking at me as though craving permission to leap on to my knees. And there he lies, his head daintily resting on my arm, as though to say: "Since you will not have me altogether, permit this at least, for I shall not disturb you if I remain so."

How mysterious is the *affection* of animals! It denotes something lofty, something superior in those natures about which we know so little.

And how well I can understand Mohammed, who, in response to the chant of the *muezzin* summoning him to prayers, cut off with a pair of scissors the hem of his cloak before rising to his feet, for fear of disturbing his cat, which had settled down thereon to sleep.

Clicker Training Step I
To Begin

How do animal trainers get cats in the movies and TV commercials to do such amazing things on cue? "Cats are impossible for me to train!" you say. Discover what the pros have known for years: a) It's not really "training"; b) you can't ask for something without paying for it; and c) all you need is a clicker and treats.

Forget command and obedience. Think that cats are independent? Well, you're wrong: They are union members, and they want to get paid for their work. It's a silent union, but a powerful one. If they feel their pay has been unfairly docked, then they will go on strike, ignoring you, exchanging looks of disdain with their comrades, and stalking off with tails and heads held high. But if you are fair, they'll be willing partners in the clicker game.

Do you have a cat who shreds the toilet paper, overturns the wastebaskets, and trashes your home on his wild rampages? Many of these undesirable behaviors are simply the result of the boredom of being housebound and getting too little interaction. Does he hide under the bed foaming at the mouth when the carrier comes out, and would you like him to learn to be "self-

Step I: To Begin

loading"? Want him to enjoy getting his claws trimmed, get off the countertop, or just plain be more active? All of this is possible.

First: Buy a Clicker

Clicker training, based on the science of operant conditioning, is so popular nowadays that you can buy clickers at any number of outlets. The sharp, precise sound of the click "marks" a behavior and signals to an animal's subconscious that she has done something right and a treat is coming. It's needed as a marker because of the timing issue: You cannot get the reward to the animal fast enough to correctly signal what it is she did right. You also can't clap your hands or say "Yes!" fast enough or sharply enough, and since these are sounds heard

Step I: To Begin

outside of training, too, they serve only to confuse your student.

Look for a clicker that emits a soft click for a cat's sound-sensitive ears, or use tape to pad a dog clicker. You can find one at your local pet supply shop or on the Internet.

Second: Practice

First, do not click your clicker near your cat's face, or near anyone's ear, for that matter. Your first session happens without the cat and is all about timing. Close yourself off in a room, sit in front of the TV, and try to click whenever you think a character is going to begin speaking. Practice clicking AS the actor opens his or her mouth, not after. You will need to be able to click during a behavior—this is harder than you think.

Third: "Charge" the Clicker

Introduce the clicker to your cat. At first, you will be using your pet's absolute favorite (preferably smelly) treat—cheese, bits of meat, human-grade tuna, peanuts—all chopped into extremely small bits, each smaller than a pea. Commercial treats may not be best, but if you use these, break each one into four or five pieces. The cat has to be able to eat each treat very quickly. This

Step I: To Begin

works for one cat or more, but you may have your hands full treating a group!

The next part is easy: Click, and hand her a treat. If she tries to steal the treats, hold them up out of the way; use a plate if they're really messy. Try to get your cat to take the treat directly from your fingers or a cupped hand; if this doesn't work, simply toss it on the floor. Wait till she downs the first bit, and then click and treat again.

If your cat walks away, let her—she either is not hungry, doesn't like your choice of treat, or is distracted. Click, hold the treat out, and wait for her to return. Don't call her or make noises. Click and treat for 20 or so repeats. By this time, the cat will understand that the click means food is coming.

Congratulations! You're on your way.

Catnip Snaps

When kitty decides that maybe he's not in the mood for his breakfast, entice him with a treat or two to start his engines. Try these tempting homemade treats to rev up your little prince or princess.

1/2 cup soy flour
3/4 cup whole wheat flour
1 1/2 teaspoons catnip
2 tablespoons wheat germ
1/3 cup powdered milk
dash salt
1 tablespoon unsulphured molasses
1 egg
2 tablespoons butter
1/3 cup cat milk (Whiskas or other brand)

1. Preheat oven to 350°F.
2. Mix together dry ingredients.
3. Add molasses, egg, butter, and milk. Mix well.
4. Mixture will be sticky. The secret to working with it is to keep wetting your rolling pin and knife. Roll it out flat onto a greased cookie sheet. Use a little extra flour if it's too sticky. With a small knife, score into very small, treat-size pieces.
5. Bake for about 15 minutes, or until crisp and brown around the edges. Let cool, break apart, and store in a sealed container in the refrigerator. Keeps for about a week.

Makes about 250 training-size treats.

A cat in distress,
Nothing more, nor less;
Good folks, I must faithfully tell ye,
As I am a sinner,
It waits for some dinner,
To stuff out its own little belly.

You would not easily guess
All the modes of distress
Which torture the tenants of earth;
And the various evils,
Which, like so many devils,
Attend the poor souls from their birth.

Some living require,
And other desire
An old fellow out of the way;
And which is best
I leave to be guessed,
For I cannot pretend to say.

One wants *society*,
Another variety,
Others a tranquil life;
Some want food,
Others, as good,
Only want a wife.

But this poor little cat
Only wanted a rat,
To stuff out its own little maw;
And it were as good
Some people had such food,
To make them *hold their jaw!*

Verses on a Cat

by Percy Bysshe Shelley

A mouse in the paws
is worth two in
the pantry.

—LOUIS WAIN

Scavenger Hunt

A Scavenger Hunt is a simple game that can involve the entire household and is hilarious to watch. It teaches your cat to depend on his sniffer—not just his eyes—to find prey objects. Stimulate your cat's "schnoz potential" by using extra-smelly treats at first. Do this before a mealtime, when Puff's a little hungry.

delicious treats, a food-oriented puss with a good sniffer

1. Close the cat in a room. Give him one tiny favorite treat to get him interested.
2. If the treats are messy, use small paper plates; otherwise, break dry treats into tiny bits. Place each bit in an obscure location: behind the TV or a wastebasket, on a shelf, under the couch—what have you. Make a note of their location so that you can pick up any leftovers.
3. Release the cat and watch the fun. If Felix is slow to catch on, place him near a treat and point him in its direction. Cats sight objects by movement, and may have trouble at first locating a stationary treat; he may pat it a couple of times to make sure it's food before eating it. Teach him to depend on his schnoz by using extra-smelly treats at first.

Waiting for Daddy

by Anonymouse

We are waiting for our daddy,
All washed, and dressed,
and nice.

We're glad, because,
We know he brings,
A basket-full
of mice.

So you've visited your local shelter, pet rescue organization, or breeder, met the perfect pet, and fallen in love. You've thought it over and are ready to welcome home your bouncing bundle of fur. Not so fast!

DON'T pick up your new charge without first setting up a good scratching post. The best ones are incorporated into a piece of multifunctional cat furniture. These allow the cat to scratch or climb to a platform or hammock that serves as a bed. Interwood Corporation and 4YourCat are two manufacturers of modular cat furniture. Or you can buy simple posts mounted on large, heavy bases that prevent wobbling. Look for stable posts taller than 30 inches and covered with sisal or jute, not carpeting. If your cat finds a really great scratching post waiting for him, there is no reason why he should choose your carpets over the post!

Arrival Day Checklist

DO find out what type of litter your new cat or kitten is accustomed to. We recommend using one with as few chemical additives as possible—especially with kittens. Set up a good-size litter tray in the room where he'll spend his first night.

DON'T plan on feeding your cat from your own dishes. Keep your china separate from your pet's (preferably stainless-steel) bowls. Pick up a stash of the food he has been eating; if you plan to make a dietary change, do it gradually.

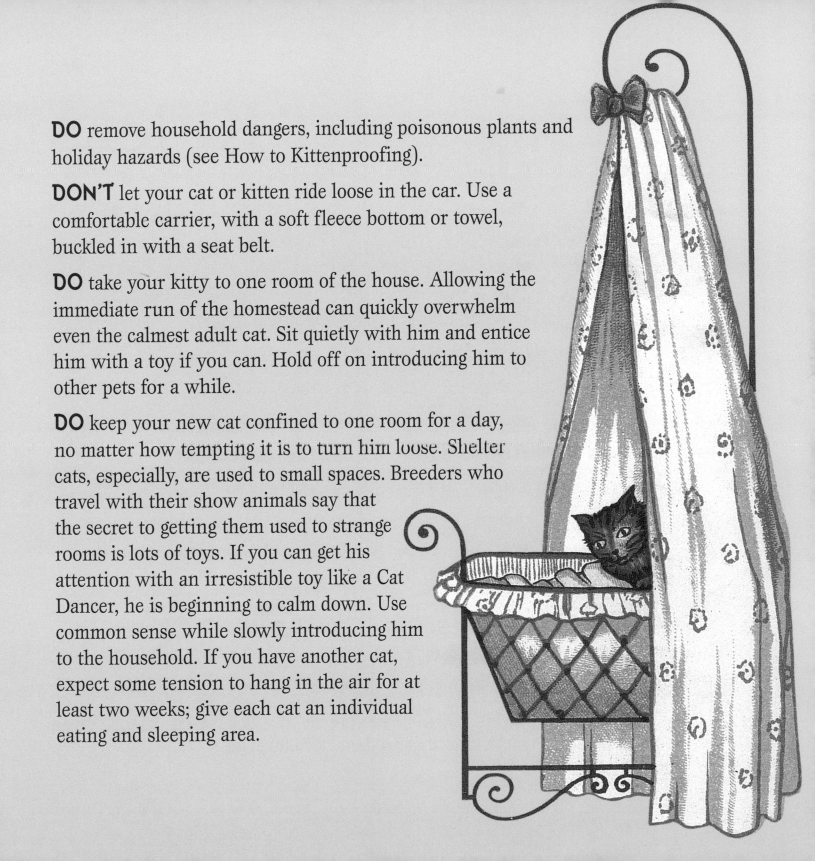

DO remove household dangers, including poisonous plants and holiday hazards (see How to Kittenproofing).

DON'T let your cat or kitten ride loose in the car. Use a comfortable carrier, with a soft fleece bottom or towel, buckled in with a seat belt.

DO take your kitty to one room of the house. Allowing the immediate run of the homestead can quickly overwhelm even the calmest adult cat. Sit quietly with him and entice him with a toy if you can. Hold off on introducing him to other pets for a while.

DO keep your new cat confined to one room for a day, no matter how tempting it is to turn him loose. Shelter cats, especially, are used to small spaces. Breeders who travel with their show animals say that the secret to getting them used to strange rooms is lots of toys. If you can get his attention with an irresistible toy like a Cat Dancer, he is beginning to calm down. Use common sense while slowly introducing him to the household. If you have another cat, expect some tension to hang in the air for at least two weeks; give each cat an individual eating and sleeping area.

Beware of Kittens

by Heinrich Heine

Beware, my friend, of fiends and their grimaces;
  Of little angels' wiles yet more beware thee;
  Just such a one to kiss her did ensnare me,
But coming, I got wounds and not embraces.
Beware of black old cats, with evil faces;
  Yet more, of kittens white and soft be wary;
  My sweetheart was just such a little fairy,
And yet she well-nigh scratched my heart to pieces.
Oh child! oh sweet love, dear beyond all measure,
  How could those eyes, so bright and clear, deceive me?
  That little paw so sore a heart-wound give me?—
My kitten's tender paw, thou soft, small treasure—
  Oh! could I to my burning lips but press thee,
  My heart the while might bleed to death and bless thee.

La Chatte Saha

by Colette

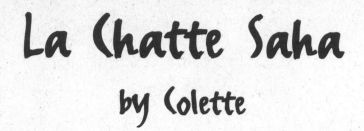

N o . . . it's you. It's you . . . you don't love me."

He backed up to the wall and pressed Camille against his hip. He could feel her shaking and cold from her shoulder to her knees, bare above the rolled stockings. She did not hold back; she yielded her whole body to him, faithfully.

"Ah, ah! I don't love you. So that's it! Another jealous scene on account of Saha?"

He could feel that whole body, pressed against his, stiffen—Camille recapturing her self-defense, her resistance; and he went on, encouraged by the moment and the opportunity.

"Instead of loving that charming animal the way I do. . . . Are we the only young married couple to bring up a cat or a dog? Would you like a parrot, a marmoset, a pair of lovebirds to make me jealous?"

She shook her shoulders and protested by making a peevish sound in her closed mouth. His head high, Alain controlled his own voice and spurred himself on.

"Come now, come on. One or two more childish bickerings, and we'll get somewhere." She's like a jar I have to turn upside down in order to empty it completely. But come on. . . .

"Would you like a little lion, a baby crocodile, say, fifty years old or so? You'd do better to adopt Saha. If you'll just take the trouble, you'll see. . . ."

Camille wrenched herself from his arms so furiously that he tottered.

"No," she cried. "That? Never. You hear what I say? Never!"

She drew a long sigh of rage and repeated in a lower tone:

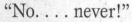

"No. . . . never!"

"That's that," he said to himself delightedly.

He pushed her into the bedroom, lowered the blinds, turned on the square ceiling lights, closed the window. With a quick movement Camille went to the window, which Alain reopened.

"On the condition that you don't scream," he said.

He rolled up the single armchair for Camille; he himself straddled the one small chair at the foot of the wide, turned-down, freshly sheeted bed. The glazed chintz curtains, drawn for the night, cast a shade of green over Camille's pallor and her crumpled white dress.

"So?" Alain began. "Impossible to settle? Horrible situation? Either she or you?"

An abrupt shake of the head was her answer and Alain was made to realize that he had better drop his bantering manner.

"What do you want me to tell you?" he began, after a silence. "The only thing I can't say? You know very well I won't give up that cat. I'd be ashamed to. Ashamed for my own sake, ashamed for her. . . ."

"I know," Camille said.

"And ashamed in your eyes," he finished.

He kept silent so long that she was angry again.

"Go on, say something. What are you waiting for?"

"The sequel," Alain said. "The end of the story."

He got up deliberately, bent over his wife, and lowered his voice as he indicated the French window.

"It was you, wasn't it? You pushed her off?"

She made a swift movement and put the bed between them, but she denied nothing.

With a kind of indulgent smile, he watched her flee.

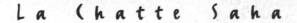

La Chatte Saha

"You threw her," he said dreamily. "I felt that you had changed everything between us. You pushed her. She broke her claws trying to catch hold of the wall . . ."

He lowered his head, seeming to picture the crime. "But how did you throw her? By clutching her by the skin of her neck? By taking advantage of her sleeping on the balcony? Have you been planning the attack for a long time? Did you two quarrel beforehand?"

He raised his head, looked at Camille's hands and arms.

"No, you haven't any marks. It was she who accused you when I asked you to touch her. She was magnificent."

He turned from Camille to look at the night, the burnt-out stars, the tops of the three poplars with the bedroom lights shining upon them.

"Well," he said simply, "I'm leaving."

"Oh, listen . . . listen . . ." Camille begged in a low voice.

But she did not hinder him from leaving the bedroom. He opened closet doors, talked to the cat in the bathroom, and from the sound of his footsteps Camille knew that he had just put on his street shoes. Mechanically she looked at the clock. He came back into the room, carrying Saha in a wide basket which Buque used when she went to market. Hastily dressed, his hair hardly combed, a handkerchief around his neck, he had the look of a lover after a quarrel. Wide eyed, Camille stared at him. But she heard Saha move in the basket and her lips tightened.

"There you are; I'm leaving," Alain said again.

He lowered his eyes, raised the basket slightly and, with designed cruelty, corrected himself:

"We're leaving."

49

There is no more intrepid
explorer than a kitten.

—JULES CHAMPFLEURY

Kittenproofing

The second you open a cupboard door, she's there. If you look away for an instant, she'll disappear, only to materialize underfoot. And just like a toddler, she puts everything in her mouth. Congratulations, you're having a kitten! Your rambunctious bundle of joy is a terror on four legs with very little sense. The following suggestions are helpful for both kitten and cat owners:

■ First, save your upholstery. Set up a wonderful scratching post before the kitten sets foot in your home. We cannot stress this enough. This way, your new addition will be trained to the post immediately, and not condition herself to use the love seat you inherited from your favorite aunt. Don't wait till after she comes home to run out to buy a post—that's too late, and you will end up with the difficult task of trying to teach a cat to stop scratching your furniture and carpets. Remember: Cats *must* scratch to groom their claws.

■ Go on "crevice patrol." Examine your baseboards and floors for holes, jagged edges, and nails. Don't allow a tiny kitten the opportunity to get in between the studs of a wall or the joists in a floor. Tape down or cover electrical cords to prevent chewing and electrical shocks.

■ Run your hand along the front baseplate of your cabinets and fill the holes. If your cabinets are on legs, is the space underneath clear enough for the kitten to get in and out easily? Can she climb up behind a unit and get stuck between it and the wall? You may have to block access to this space with heavy cardboard or wood until your kitten is larger and smarter.

53

■ Next, open the doors of all base cabinets and run your hand along the backs at the bottom. Is there a space at the floor between the cabinet and the wall that a kitten could fit into and, from there, jam herself under the base? Examine the interiors of wall cabinets, too, for any holes. Make sure your kitten can't climb through and end up behind a wall panel between upper and lower cabinets.

■ Block off fireplaces, attic, and other off-limits areas. Kittens won't hesitate to climb partway up the inside of a chimney and get covered with creosote; this requires an emergency vet visit and detergents. Remind family members that certain doors must always be kept shut (hang signs, if necessary). Put lids on toilet seats down; kittens are prone to falling in.

■ Place all household cleaners, tools, garbage, medicines, and sharp equipment in off-limits locations. Mothballs and phenols found in some disinfectants are toxic. Antifreeze actually attracts dogs and cats with its sweet flavor, and will kill them. Get rid of poisonous plants and holiday hazards.

■ Remove knickknacks from open surfaces. Don't leave items that a kitten could swallow lying around.

■ Examine commercial pet toys and remove any decorations that your pet could chew off and swallow.

■ Thread, fishing line, and dental floss are strictly off-limits for cats of any age. If swallowed, these can wrap themselves around a section of intestine and require emergency surgery to save your pet's life. Some cats have a compulsion to swallow wool yarn. Use string or twine for supervised playtime.

■ Finally, monitor a kitten carefully the first day you give her run of the house. Note her personality traits and unique brand of mischief. Keep her bed, litter box, post, food, and toys in an area that you can close off, like a den or bedroom, in case you have to leave her alone. Enjoy! Kittenhood is gone in a flash.

Kitty Foosball

Have a bored cat? Watch her come alive for this challenge. It's a little like foosball with paws. Cats peer through the top, figuring out how to get the toys out, while reaching in through the side holes to bat them around. It can busy them for hours if the holes are too small to get the objects out easily. While store-bought versions are available, we recommend making this model first.

rectangular, shallow cardboard boxes (like the type used for cat food cans or file folders); utility or X-Acto knife; small items such as Ping-Pong balls, catnip toys, sparkle balls, etc.; strapping tape

1. Use the top and bottom of an office-supply box or two cat-food-can cases to make a top that fits over a bottom. Cut two holes in each short end of the top box, just big enough to poke a Ping-Pong ball through. Cut three holes in each long edge. Cut three rows of two holes each in the top.

2. Place the top over the bottom and trace the holes on the sides of the bottom box; cut these out so that holes go all the way through. Load the box with five or six toys (Ping-Pong balls and small catnip toys are great) and close it. Tape the bottom and top together securely, reinforcing it with tape so it won't collapse if your cat jumps on top of it.

How Many?

So you've brought home a new cat or kitten and are wondering whether he must have a playmate in order not to be lonely. Behaviorists who have studied feral cat colonies for years still answer this question with a no. Dogs kept from other dogs usually have some issues, whereas cats do not require the companionship of their own species. Although small cats in groups learn to tolerate and even greet each other to keep the peace, they hunt alone, are not pack animals like dogs, and display competitive, not cooperative, behavior. Lion prides are the only cat groups that cooperate, and only because they hunt very large prey.

There is, of course, nothing wrong with having more than one cat; even house cats need their space, or territory, however, and will display jealousy to varying degrees—sometimes arguing over who gets to sleep closest to the human. And bathing each other can turn inexplicably into a spat, and then turn just as inexplicably into a communal nap. How many cats are too many? This varies with the household, and the disposition of the particular cats, but vets seem to agree that as a general rule of thumb, keeping four cats in a city apartment is getting close to the borderline.

O nce upon a time, and long, long ago, a little boy was left in the care of a group of monks at a temple in the country- side. In a short time, the monks learned that there was one thing this boy loved to do above all else, and that was draw. His skill was extraordinary, and so to encourage him, the monks allowed him the free- dom to draw anything he liked. And the things he loved to draw above all else were cats.

The Boy Who Drew Cats

A Japanese Legend

Maybe they allowed him too much freedom, for as he got older, they realized that his drawing was growing out of control. Instead of restraining his artwork to parchment, his beautiful creations were sprawled across walls, etched into screens, and even displayed on the floor! Everywhere one turned, small cats peeked out from corners, large cats stretched beneath windows, cats with fierce eyes glared at meek cats gently cleaning themselves on rice paper screens. The monks began to complain.

"Our temple should be a place of simplicity and purity. How can one worship if everywhere we look, there are cats ready to spring at us?" one asked.

The eldest monk of the temple shook his head. "This will not do. The boy must learn some restraint." And so he called the boy to him.

"My boy, you have lived with us for many years. We have all seen your talent grow from a tiny seed into a beautiful flower." The boy blushed with pride and gently stroked a paintbrush he was holding, "But your paintings are disrupting the routine of our fellow monks."

"I don't understand. Don't you like my pictures?" the boy asked.

The elder sighed, "Yes. But it apparent to me that your talent is becoming chaotic. Perhaps you have been confined to this temple for too long. I feel that is best for you to travel out into the world. Maybe then you will find a way to focus your art."

The boy was sad to hear that the elder wanted him to leave, but at the same time, a tiny flame of excitement flickered within his heart. He had always wondered what lay beyond the grounds of the temple, and now he would finally get his chance to find out!

After saying his good-byes and packing his few belongings, including his precious paintbrushes and ink, the boy set off into the countryside. He walked for miles and miles, but hardly seemed tired. He had never been this far from the temple before and everything he saw seemed new and wonderful to him.

"I could stop and stay here for the rest of my life, and still not run out of things to paint," he declared as he took in the view from a gently rolling hill.

CAT TALES

But as eager as he was to see what lay just beyond the next rise, dusk soon began to fall, and the boy realized he needed to find shelter for the night. He had just made his way through a thick grove of trees, when suddenly he saw a large temple sitting atop a hill.

"The monks will gladly let me stay there for the night," he thought and made his way towards the large structure.

But as he got closer, he saw that the temple grounds were in great disrepair. After knocking at the door and getting no answer, the boy let himself into the temple, and discovered that it had not been used in some time.

"I wonder why that is," he murmured. But the mystery was pushed out of his head when he lit a lamp and saw that the walls of the temple were a beautiful, smooth white. It looked exactly like one giant canvas, and the boy gasped at the possibilities.

He quickly set up his paintbrush and ink, and began drawing on every square inch of available space. He painted coy cats with curlicue tails, and sweet cats with velvety eyes. He didn't stop until all of the walls had been covered by one hundred different felines in one hundred different poses. After such a grand undertaking, he was exhausted and eagerly made a bed

CAT TALES

CAT TALES

on the temple floor. But after lying down, he found that he could not sleep.

He tossed and turned, and turned and tossed, and finally gathered up his blankets.

"I don't know why it is, but this room makes me very uneasy," he thought, and after investigating the rest of the temple, he found a small closet to the side of the main room, The boy arranged his bed inside that and gently closed the door.

No sooner had his eyes shut, when a terrible snarl came from outside. Petrified with fear, the boy lay frozen in the dark as the horrible sound echoed again and again. Suddenly, he heard a loud thumping noise, accompanied by a chorus of howls and screams. It sounded as if a ferocious battle was taking place right outside the closet door, but the boy was too scared to even peek out! He listened to the gruesome noises for what seemed like hours, until, suddenly, after one final, agonizing scream, the room fell silent. The boy shook in his bed and waited desperately for the dawn to come.

When a tiny sliver of light finally slipped under the closet door, the boy gathered up his courage and slowly stepped out into the main room.

CAT TALES

There he discovered the lifeless body of a hideous rat, the size of a small horse, lying in the middle of the room!

Such a disgusting rat would have snapped him right in two if he had slept in the main room the night before, and the thought made him weak. But what had saved him from such a horrible fate and vanquished this terrible enemy? He looked around the room, and although he found signs of a battle, he could see no weapons of any kind.

The boy was about to gather his things and leave as fast his legs could carry him, when he noticed that one of his painted cats appeared to have a red circle around his mouth.

"But I have no red paint," the boy thought. He slowly examined his other paintings, and discovered that other cats seemed to have bits of fur stuck to the wall where their claws were drawn. In fact, now that he looked closely, all of the cats seemed to be in completely different positions than before!

"Could it be that my painted cats have saved me?" the boy wondered. Silently thanking his wonderful creations, he gathered his things and left the temple as fast as he could. After walking a short distance, he came to a village and explained what had happened at the first shop he came to.

"You mean you've killed the demon of the temple?" the shopkeeper exclaimed. He quickly spread the news, and the villagers gathered and told the boy that for as long as anyone could remember, a monstrous demon that took the shape of a giant rat had plagued the temple, making it impossible for the villagers to worship. When they realized their ancient enemy was now defeated, they cheered and carried the boy on their shoulders throughout the village, proclaiming him a hero.

The boy never discovered how his magical drawings had saved him that night, but he did believe that his art had rescued him from a terrible fate. As he grew older, the boy learned to draw other things, and he became a famous artist throughout the land. It was said that his pictures seemed so real, so lifelike, they might someday jump right off the canvas.

But none were more realistic than the hundred cats he drew that night in the temple, long, long ago.

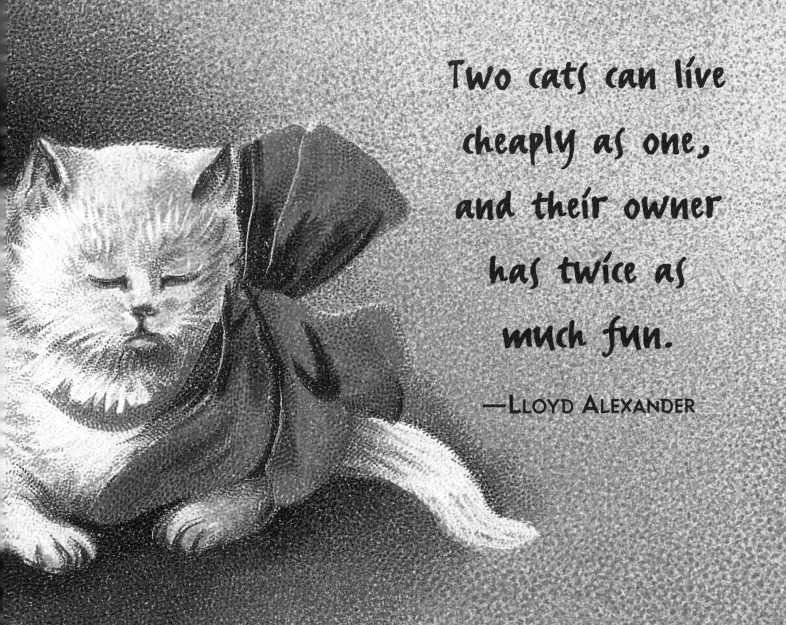

Two cats can live cheaply as one, and their owner has twice as much fun.

—LLOYD ALEXANDER

Clicker Training Step 2
The Touch

The final goal of the Touch is to get the cat to press her nose to the end of the prop. It's a basic building block for other training. During this first trick, both you and your cat will be learning. Very experienced trainers can teach a "green" cat a new behavior in a matter of minutes.

clicker (see page 29), 20–30 treats, chopstick or plastic straw

1. Prepare to click immediately. Hold the stick about 2 or 3 inches from your cat's face. As—not *after*—he looks at it, click, and then treat. Don't wiggle the prop around. Don't touch him with it or make noises.
2. If she paws or bites the prop, don't click; withdraw it for a few seconds and slowly hold it out again. She will realize eventually that out-of-control pawing will not get her the treats she smells.
3. Click each time the cat makes the tiniest head motion toward the stick, and then treat. Don't ask for perfection. Treat, then repeat. He will soon figure out that he's "getting paid" for doing a very simple thing.
4. You may get lucky: Your cat may touch the prop with her nose right away. *CLICK!* Hit that clicker while it is happening,

and before kitty paws it or does something else you don't want, hand her two treats (reinforcements) to let her know "That's IT!"

5. After 20 or so treats, put the clicker, prop, and treats away till another session. Don't leave items out, or kitty can get the idea that they are toys.

6. It could take a couple of sessions per day over a week, each involving 20 treats, or it may happen sooner. Once your cat "gets it" (this is called *startling*) and is repeating the behavior, try presenting the prop slightly to one side and then the other. Click the instant his head follows. Try to increase the repetition speed, then the distance you hold the prop away. Back up and start over if he walks away, begins rubbing everything, or appears to forget.

7. Eventually begin adding the verbal cue, "Touch," just before the cat touches the prop.

Once you've gotten some fairly consistent results over several days, your cat will get excited the moment the prop and clicker come out. You now have a "clicker-wise" pet!

CAT TALES

Once upon a time, a man was given a cat as a birthday present. The feline was a beautiful dark grey with bright, sparkling eyes and a patch of white at its throat.

"Such a handsome cat deserves a very fine name!" the man declared to the party guests, as he stroked its soft head.

"You should name him Tiger!" suggested one guest, "That way he will be as fierce as a tiger when it comes to fighting battles in the alley!"

"Nonsense," another interrupted. "You should name him Dragon. He will possess the strength of ten tigers, as well as a noble temperament to boot."

A third guest bent to scoop the cat up in her arms. "Why not name him Cloud? Clouds are strong enough for even dragons to lie on, and they are as graceful as a flock of butterflies."

What's In a Name?

A Chinese Folktale

"Pshaw," a portly guest added, "but what moves the clouds to its whim? Why, the wind, of course!" He reached over to pet the cat and continued, "Call this cat Wind and he

CAT TALES

will be as wily and playful as the invisible breezes!"

"The winds are indeed crafty," another friend said as the cat leapt out of the lady's arms, "and there's only one thing that can stop them: a wall. A cat named Wall will be as steadfast as brick and as sure as granite."

"My friends," said one other guest, who perhaps had had a bit too much to drink, "all of these are wonderful suggestions. All walls are very difficult to overcome. But," here he raised a swaying finger, "what is the one thing that can find its way through a wall as easily as water? Why, a mouse, of course! Call it Mouse!"

"Oh, for heaven's sake," the host bellowed, as the party broke out in laughter. "A cat will be graceful and strong, fierce and playful, steadfast and clever with any name. After all, a cat is a cat no matter what I call it. So why on earth should I name it anything else?"

And Cat seemed to think this was very wise indeed.

Cheesy Treats

Especially for critters with a "cheese" tooth, these tasty wonders are made with all human-grade ingredients from your pantry. Every member of the family, feline and otherwise, can enjoy Cheesy Treats. So, don't be surprised if you find a hand in the cheesy jar!

1 cup flour
1/2 cup cornmeal
1 egg, beaten
1/4 cup water
2/3 cup grated Parmesan cheese, divided
sprinkling of salt

1. Preheat the oven to 300°F.
2. Combine all the ingredients except half the cheese. Flour your hands and knead until thoroughly mixed.
3. On a floured surface, roll the dough into long, thin "worms" with floured hands. Pull apart into 1-inch pieces.
4. Roll the pieces in the remaining cheese and place them on a greased baking sheet.
5. Bake for 10–12 minutes. Store in a sealed container in the fridge for up to 2 weeks. These can be broken apart into cheesy kibble-size treats.

Makes about 4 cups.

Calvin

by Charles Dudley Warner

Calvin is dead. His life, long to him, but short for the rest of us, was not marked by startling adventures, but his character was so uncommon and his qualities were so worthy of imitation, that I have been asked by those who personally knew him to set down my recollections of his career.

His origin and ancestry were shrouded in mystery; even his age was a matter of pure conjecture. Although he was of the Maltese race, I have reason to suppose that he was American by birth as he certainly was in sympathy. Calvin was given to me eight years ago by Mrs. Stowe, but she knew nothing of his age or origin. He walked into her house one day out of the great unknown and became at once at home, as if he had been always a friend of the family. He appeared to have artistic and literary tastes, and it was as if he had inquired at the door if that was the residence of the author of *Uncle Tom's Cabin*, and, upon being assured that it was, had decided to dwell there. This is, of course, fanciful, for his antecedents were wholly unknown, but in his time he could hardly have been in any household where he would not have heard *Uncle Tom's Cabin* talked about. When he came to Mrs. Stowe, he was as large as he ever was, and apparently as old as he ever became. Yet there was in him no appearance of age; he was in the happy maturity of all his powers, and you would rather have said that in that maturity he had found the secret of perpetual youth. And it was as difficult to believe that he would ever be aged as it was to imagine that he had ever been in immature youth. There was in him a mysterious perpetuity.

After some years, when Mrs. Stowe made her winter home in Florida, Calvin came to live with us. From the first moment, he fell into the ways of the house and assumed a recognized position in the family,—I say recognized, because after he became known he was always inquired for by visitors, and in the letters to the other members of the family he always received a message. Although the least obtrusive of beings, his individuality always made itself felt.

His personal appearance had much to do with this, for he was of royal mold, and had an air of high breeding. He was large, but he had nothing of the fat grossness of the celebrated Angora family; though powerful, he was exquisitely proportioned, and as graceful in every movement as a young leopard. When he stood up to open a door—he opened all the doors with old-fashioned latches—he was portentously tall, and when stretched on the rug before the fire he seemed too long for this world— as indeed he was. His coat was the finest and softest I have ever seen, a shade of quiet Maltese; and from his throat downward, underneath, to the white tips of his feet, he wore the whitest and most delicate ermine; and no person was ever more fastidiously neat. In his finely formed head you saw something of his aristocratic character; the ears were small and cleanly cut, there was a tinge of pink in the nostrils, his face was handsome, and the expression of his countenance exceedingly intelligent—I should call it even a sweet expression if the term were not inconsistent with his look of alertness and sagacity.

Calvin

It is difficult to convey a just idea of his gayety in connection with his dignity and gravity, which his name expressed. As we know nothing of his family, of course it will be understood that Calvin was his Christian name. He had times of relaxation into utter playfulness, delighting in a ball of yarn, catching sportively at stray ribbons when his mistress was at her toilet, and pursuing his own tail, with hilarity, for lack of anything better. He could amuse himself by the hour, and he did not care for children; perhaps something in his past was present to his memory. He had absolutely no bad habits, and his disposition was perfect. I never saw him exactly angry, though I have seen his tail grow to an enormous size when a strange cat appeared upon his lawn. He disliked cats, evidently regarding them as feline and treacherous, and he had no association with them. Occasionally there would be heard a night concert in the shrubbery. Calvin would ask to have the door opened, and then you would hear a rush and a "pestzt," and the concert would explode, and Calvin would quietly come in and resume his seat on the hearth. There was no trace of anger in his manner, but he wouldn't have any of that about the house. He had the rare virtue of magnanimity.

Although he had fixed notions about his own rights, and extraordinary persistency in getting them, he never showed temper at a repulse; he simply and firmly persisted till he had what he wanted. His diet was one point; his idea was that of the scholars about dictionaries—to "get the best." He knew as well as anyone what was in the house, and would refuse beef if turkey was to be had; and if there were oysters, he would wait over the turkey to see if the oysters would not be forthcoming. And yet he was not a gross gourmand; he would eat bread if he saw me eating it, and thought he was not being imposed on. His habits of feeding, also, were refined; he never used a knife, and he would put up his hand and draw the fork down to his mouth as grace-fully as a grown person. Unless necessity compelled, he would not eat in the kitchen, but insisted upon his meals in the dining-room, and would wait patiently, unless a stranger were present; and then he was sure to importune the visitor, hoping that the latter was ignorant of the rule of the house, and would give him something. They used to say that he pre-ferred as his tablecloth on the floor a certain well-known church journal;

but this was said by an Episcopalian. So far as I know, he had no religious prejudices, except that he did not like the association with Romanists. He tolerated the servants, because they belonged to the house, and would sometimes linger by the kitchen stove; but the moment visitors came in he arose, opened the door, and marched into the drawing-room. Yet he enjoyed the company of his equals, and never withdrew, no matter how many callers—whom he recognized as of his society—might come into the drawing-room. Calvin was fond of company, but he wanted to choose it; and I have no doubt that his was an aristocratic fastidiousness rather than one of faith. It is so with most people.

The intelligence of Calvin was something phenomenal, in his rank of life. He established a method of communicating his wants, and even some of his sentiments; and he could help himself in many things. There was a furnace register in a retired room, where he used to go when he wished to be alone, that he always opened when he desired more heat; but never shut it, any more than he shut the door after himself. He could do almost everything but speak; and you would declare sometimes that you could see a pathetic longing to do that in his intelligent face. I have no desire to overdraw his qualities, but if there was one thing in him more noticeable than another, it was his fondness for nature. He could content himself for hours at a low window, looking into the ravine and at the great trees, noting the smallest stir there; he delighted, above all things, to accompany me walking about the garden, hearing the birds, getting the smell of the fresh earth, and rejoicing in the sunshine. He

Calvin

followed me and gamboled like a dog, rolling over on the turf and exhibiting his delight in a hundred ways. If I worked, he sat and watched me, or looked off over the bank, and kept his ear open to the twitter in the cherry trees. When it stormed, he was sure to sit at the window, keenly watching the rain or the snow, glancing up and down at its falling; and a winter tempest always delighted him. I think he was genuinely fond of birds, but, so far as I know, he usually confined himself to one a day; he never killed, as some sportsmen do, for the sake of killing, but only as civilized people do—from necessity. He was intimate with the flying squirrels who dwell in the chestnut trees—too intimate, for almost every day in the summer he would bring in one, until he nearly discouraged them. He was, indeed, a superb hunter, and would have been a devastating one, if his bump of destructiveness had not been offset by a bump of moderation. There was very little of the brutality of the lower animals about him; I don't think he enjoyed rats for themselves, but he knew his business, and for the first few months of his residence with us he waged an awful campaign against the horde, and after that his simple presence was sufficient to deter them from coming on the premises. Mice amused him, but he usually considered them too small game to be taken seriously; I have seen him play for an hour with a mouse, and then let him go with a royal condescension. In this whole matter of "getting a living," Calvin was a great contrast to the rapacity of the age in which he lived.

I hesitate a little to speak of his capacity for friendship and the affectionateness of his nature, for I know from his own reserve that he would not care to have it much talked about. We understood each other perfectly,

84

but we never made any fuss about it; when I spoke his name and snapped my fingers, he came to me; when I returned home at night, he was pretty sure to be waiting for me near the gate, and would rise and saunter along the walk, as if his being there were purely accidental,—so shy was he commonly of showing feeling; and when I opened the door he never rushed in, like a cat, but loitered, and lounged, as if he had had no intention of going in, but would con-descend to. And yet, the fact was, he knew din-ner was ready, and he was bound to be there. He kept the run of dinner-time. It happened sometimes, during our absence in the summer, that dinner would be early, and Calvin, walking about the grounds, missed it and came in late. But he never made a mistake the second day. There was one thing he never did,—he never rushed through an open doorway. He never forgot his dig-nity. If he had asked to have the door opened, and was eager to go out, he always went deliberately; I can see him now, standing on the sill, looking about at the sky as if he was thinking whether it were worth while to take an umbrella, until he was near having his tail shut in.

His friendship was rather constant than demonstra-tive. When we returned from an absence of nearly two years, Calvin welcomed us with evident pleasure, but

Calvin

showed his satisfaction rather by tranquil happiness than by fuming
about. He had the faculty of making us glad to get home. It was his con-
stancy that was so attractive. He liked companionship, but he wouldn't
be petted, or fussed over, or sit in any one's lap a moment; he always
extricated himself from such familiarity with dignity and with no show
of temper. If there was any petting to be done, however, he chose to do
it. Often he would sit looking at me, and then, moved by a delicate affection, come and pull at my coat and sleeve until he could touch my face
with his nose, and then go away contented. He had a habit of coming to
my study in the morning, sitting quietly by my side or on the table for
hours, watching the pen run over the paper, occasionally swinging his
tail round for a blotter, and then going to sleep among the papers by the
inkstand. Or, more rarely, he would watch the writing from a perch on
my shoulder. Writing always interested him, and, until he understood it,
he wanted to hold the pen.

He always held himself in a kind of reserve with his friend, as if he
had said, "Let us respect our personality, and not make a 'mess' of
friendship." He saw, with Emerson, the risk of degrading it to trivial con-
veniency. "Why insist on rash personal relations with your friend?"
"Leave this touching and clawing." Yet I would not give an unfair notion
of his aloofness, his fine sense of the sacredness of the me and the not-
me. And, at the risk of not being believed, I will relate an incident, which
was often repeated. Calvin had the practice of passing a portion of the
night in the contemplation of its beauties, and would come into our

87

chamber over the roof of the conservatory through the open window, summer and winter, and go to sleep on the foot of my bed. He would do this always exactly in this way; he never was content to stay in the chamber if we compelled him to go upstairs and through the door. He had the obstinacy of General Grant. But this is by the way. In the morning, he performed his toilet and went down to breakfast with the rest of the family. Now, when the mistress was absent from home, and at no other time, Calvin would come in the morning, when the bell rang, to the head of the bed, put up his feet and look into my face, follow me about when I rose, "assist" at the dressing, and in many purring ways show his fondness, as if he had plainly said, "I know that she has gone away, but I am here." Such was Calvin in rare moments.

He had his limitations. Whatever passion he had for nature, he had no conception of art. There was sent to him once a fine and very expressive cat's head in bronze, by Frémiet. I placed it on the floor. He regarded it intently, approached it cautiously and crouchingly, touched it with his nose, perceived the fraud, turned away abruptly, and never would notice it afterward. On the whole, his life was not only a successful one, but a happy one. He never had but one fear, so far as I know: he had a mortal and a reasonable terror of plumbers. He would never stay in the house when they were here. No coaxing could quiet him. Of course he didn't share our fear about their charges, but he must have had some dreadful experience with them in that portion of his life which is unknown to us. A plumber was to him the devil, and I have no doubt that, in his scheme, plumbers were foreordained to do him mischief.

Calvin

In speaking of his worth, it has never occurred to me to estimate Calvin by the worldly standard. I know that it is customary now, when anyone dies, to ask how much he was worth, and that no obituary in the newspapers is considered complete without such an estimate. The plumbers in our house were one day overheard to say that, "They say that *she* says that *he* says that he wouldn't take a hundred dollars for him." It is unnecessary to say that I never made such a remark, and that, so far as Calvin was concerned, there was no purchase in money.

As I look back upon it, Calvin's life seems to me a fortunate one, for it was natural and unforced. He ate when he was hungry, slept when he was sleepy, and enjoyed existence to the very tips of his toes and the end of his expressive and slow-moving tail. He delighted to roam about the garden, and stroll among the trees, and to lie on the green grass and

Calvin

luxuriate in all the sweet influences of summer. You could never accuse him of idleness, and yet he knew the secret of repose. The poet who wrote so prettily of him that his little life was rounded with a sleep, understated his felicity; it was rounded with a good many. His conscience never seemed to interfere with his slumbers. In fact, he had good habits and a contented mind. I can see him now walk in at the study door, sit down by my chair, bring his tail artistically about his feet, and look up at me with unspeakable happiness in his handsome face. I often thought that he felt the dumb limitation which denied him the power of language. But since he was denied speech, he scorned the inarticulate mouthings of the lower animals. The vulgar mewing and yowling of the cat species was beneath him; he sometimes uttered a sort of articulate and well-bred ejaculation, when he wished to call attention to something that he considered remarkable, or to some want of his, but he never went whining about. He would sit for hours at a closed window, when he desired to enter, without a murmur, and when it was opened he never admitted that he had been impatient by "bolting" in. Though speech he had not, and the unpleasant kind of utterance given to his race he would not use, he had a mighty power of purr to express his measureless content with congenial society. There was in him a musical organ with stops of varied power and expression, upon which I have no doubt he could have performed Scarlatti's celebrated cat's-fugue.

Whether Calvin died of old age, or was carried off by one of the diseases incident to youth, it is impossible to say; for his departure was as quiet as his advent was mysterious. I only know that he appeared to us

92

in this world in his perfect stature and beauty, and that after a time, like Lohengrin, he withdrew. In his illness there was nothing more to be regretted than in all his blameless life. I suppose there never was an illness that had more of dignity and sweetness and resignation in it. It came on gradually, in a kind of listlessness and want of appetite. An alarming symptom was his preference for the warmth of a furnace-register to the lively sparkle of the open wood-fire. Whatever pain he suffered, he bore it in silence, and seemed only anxious not to obtrude his malady. We tempted him with the delicacies of the season, but it soon became impossible for him to eat, and for two weeks he ate or drank scarcely anything.

Sometimes he made an effort to take something, but it was evident that he made the effort to please us. The neighbors—and I am convinced that the advice of neighbors is never good for anything—suggested catnip. He wouldn't even smell it. We had the attendance of an amateur practitioner of medicine, whose real office was the cure of souls, but nothing touched his case. He took what was offered, but it was with the air of one to whom the time for pellets was past. He sat or lay day after day almost motionless, never once making a display of those vulgar convulsions or contortions of pain which are so disagreeable to society. His favorite place was on the brightest spot of a Smyrna rug by the conservatory, where the sunlight fell and he could hear the fountain play. If we went to him and exhibited our interest in his condition, he always purred in recognition of our

Calvin

sympathy. And when I spoke his name, he looked up with an expression that said, "I understand it, old fellow, but it's no use." He was to all who came to visit him a model of calmness and patience in affliction.

I was absent from home at the last, but heard by daily postal-card of his failing condition; and never again saw him alive. One sunny morning, he rose from his rug, went into the conservatory (he was very thin then), walked around it deliberately, looking at all the plants he knew, and then went to the bay-window in the dining-room, and stood a long time looking out upon the little field, now brown and sere, and toward the garden, where perhaps the happiest hours of his life had been spent. It was a last look. He turned and walked away, laid himself down upon the bright spot in the rug, and quietly died.

It is not too much to say that a little shock went through the neighborhood when it was known that Calvin was dead, so marked was his individuality; and his friends, one after another, came in to see him. There was no sentimental nonsense about his obsequies; it was felt that any parade would have been distasteful to him. John, who acted as undertaker, prepared a candle-box for him, and I believe assumed a professional decorum; but there may have been the usual levity underneath, for I heard that he remarked in the kitchen that it was the "dryest wake he ever attended." Everybody, however, felt a fondness for Calvin, and regarded him with a certain respect. Between him and Bertha there existed a great friendship, and she apprehended his nature; she used to say that sometimes she was afraid of him, he looked at her so intelligently; she was never certain that he was what he appeared to be.

When I returned, they had laid Calvin on a table in an upper chamber by an open window. It was February. He reposed in a candle-box, lined about the edge with evergreen, and at his head stood a little wine-glass with flowers. He lay with his head tucked down in his arms—a favorite position of his before the fire—as if asleep in the comfort of his soft and exquisite fur. It was the involuntary exclamation of those who saw him, "How natural he looks!" As for myself, I said nothing. John buried him under the twin hawthorn-trees—one white and the other pink—in a spot where Calvin was fond of lying and listening to the hum of summer insects and the twitter of birds.

Perhaps I have failed to make appear the individuality of character that was so evident to those who knew him. At any rate, I have set down nothing concerning him but the literal truth. He was always a mystery. I did not know whence he came; I do not know whither he has gone. I would not weave one spray of falsehood in the wreath I lay upon his grave.

Catnip Sock

You've seen them in the stores: dozens of catnip toys, catnip mice, even stuffed catnip vegetables. Don't be fooled by all the decorations and high prices. This old standby, the shapeless, lowly, homemade catnip sock may win first place in Most Mutilated Toy category. Cats love to sink teeth and claws into the soft, plush cotton knit. Don't be surprised if your furry friend carries it off to his "secret place."

Child's crew sock, scissors, needle and thread, elastic hair band, tissue paper, catnip

1. Depending on the size of the sock, cut the toe or foot section off and discard the cuff; otherwise, the toy will be too big.
2. Turn the toe section wrong-side out. Place the elastic around the top edge. Fold over the edge to cover the band, as with a drawstring waistband, and stitch the edge securely. The casing makes a sturdier toy, and will prevent a rambunctious puss from pulling the elastic band off.
3. Snip a small rectangular notch out of the top edge. This will serve as a small opening for access to the elastic. Stitch around the edges of the notch so they don't fray. Turn the sock-bag right-side out and stuff with tissue paper and catnip.
4. Pull the elastic through the notch and loop it tightly around the top several times, like a rubber band around a ponytail, until it is very tight. Toss!
5. Replenish catnip as needed.

There was once a merchant who, crossing the vast desert, stopped at an oasis to refresh himself. As he came to the still water, he discovered two robbers that were beating and robbing a man. The merchant immediately entered the fray, and managed to fight off the attackers, sending them running across the burning sands. He examined the barely conscious man, tended to his injuries, provided him with food, and shared his fire with him that night.

After the wounded man had recovered enough to be able to sit up and speak, he sat beside the merchant. The campfire glowed beneath the black skies, and for a while, neither man spoke. The fire flickered and danced, sending shadows across the smooth sands. Finally, the wounded man began, "Thank you for helping me. Those robbers came upon me by surprise as I was resting."

A Cat Made of Magic

A Tale from Ancient Persia

CAT TALES

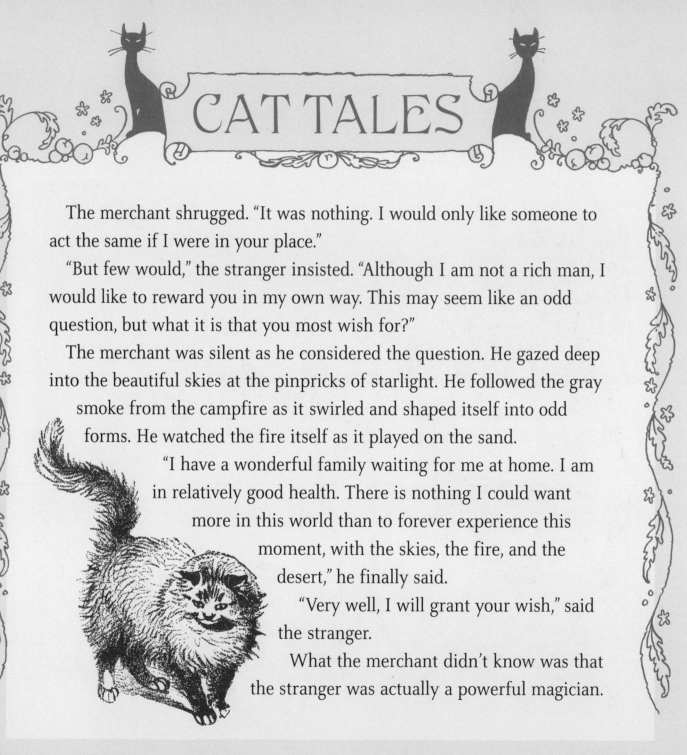

The merchant shrugged. "It was nothing. I would only like someone to act the same if I were in your place."

"But few would," the stranger insisted. "Although I am not a rich man, I would like to reward you in my own way. This may seem like an odd question, but what it is that you most wish for?"

The merchant was silent as he considered the question. He gazed deep into the beautiful skies at the pinpricks of starlight. He followed the gray smoke from the campfire as it swirled and shaped itself into odd forms. He watched the fire itself as it played on the sand.

"I have a wonderful family waiting for me at home. I am in relatively good health. There is nothing I could want more in this world than to forever experience this moment, with the skies, the fire, and the desert," he finally said.

"Very well, I will grant your wish," said the stranger.

What the merchant didn't know was that the stranger was actually a powerful magician.

With a low chant, he deftly gathered the smoke from the fire into a ball which he cupped in one hand. He reached up and smoothly plucked two stars from the ebony sky. He pulled a bit of flame from the campfire, and finally, he gathered a pinch of sand into his closed fist.

"Amazing," the merchant whispered.

The merchant couldn't quite tell what the magician did next, but it seemed as if he was molding something with these extraordinary objects, as one would with clay. After several moments of breathless anticipation, a faint sound drifted across the sand.

Out of the magician's powerful hands slipped a beautiful long-haired cat with fur the color of smoke, eyes as bright as stars that danced with a hidden flame, and (when she dainty licked the merchant's hand), a tongue as gritty as the sands of the desert!

The magician handed him the creature and said, "This cat is the perfect embodiment of all that you treasure at this moment. Take good care of her and you will never lose the memory." The merchant thanked the magician and took the magical cat home. And so, the Persian cat was created in this world.

Among animals, cats are
the top-hatted, frock-coated
statesmen going about their
affairs at their own pace.

—ROBERT STEARNS

Draggin' Dragon

The Cat Dancer (which makes a soft whirring sound), the beaded mouse (which rattles), and the Crinkle Sack, three of the most popular commercial cat toys around, owe their success in part to cats' love of all things rustly. This activity does, too. Most cats find chasing the dragon "irresistable," yet there are a few who react with the equivalent of "We are not amused." If your cat is at first afraid of it, lay it on the floor and let her sniff it over.

4–5 yards crinkly brown paper (like brown packaging paper but lighter in weight, yet heavier than ordinary tissue paper; find it at a packing or art supply store), scissors

1. Clear some space (say, a 30-foot run) so you won't be crashing into the furniture.

2. Crush the crinkly paper together lengthwise. Tie one knot in the middle and one knot about a foot from each end of the Dragon.

3. At one end, use the scissors to cut a fringe for the tail.

4. Grab the knot at the other end, or tie that end around your child's waist. Walk quickly with the Dragon trailing out behind you. Most cats love attacking the end, and even being gently dragged across the carpet.

Stately, kindly, lordly friend,
   Condescend
Here to sit by me, and turn
Glorious eyes that smile and burn,
Golden eyes, love's lustrous meed,
On the golden page I read.

All your wondrous wealth of hair,
   Dark and fair,
Silken-shaggy, soft and bright
As the clouds and beams of night,
Pays my reverent hand's caress
Back with friendlier gentleness.

Dogs may fawn on all and some,
   As they come;
You, a friend of loftier mind,
Answer friends alone in kind;
Just your foot upon my hand
Softly bids it understand.

Wild on woodland ways, your sires
   Flashed like fires;
Fair as flame, and fierce, and fleet,

To a Cat

by Algernon Charles Swinburne

As with wings on wingless feet,
Shone and sprang your mother, free,
Bright and brave as wind or sea.

Free, and proud, and glad as they,
    Here to-day
Rests or roams their radiant child,
Vanquished not, but reconciled;
Free from curb of aught above
Save the lovely curb of love.

Love, through dreams of souls divine,
    Fain would shine
Round a dawn whose light and song
Then should right our mutual wrong,—
Speak, and seal the love-lit law,
Sweet Assisi's seer foresaw.

Dreams were theirs; yet haply may
    Dawn a day
When such friends and fellows born,
Seeing our earth as fair at morn,
May, for wiser love's sake, see
More of heaven's deep heart than we.

I have added a romantic inmate to my family,—a large bloodhound, allowed to be the finest dog of the kind in Scotland, perfectly gentle, affectionate, good-natured, and the darling of all the children. He is between the deer-greyhound and mastiff, with a shaggy mane like a lion, and always sits beside me at dinner, his head as high as the back of my chair; yet it will gratify you to know that a favorite cat keeps him in the greatest possible order, insists upon all rights of precedence, and scratches with impunity the nose of an animal who would make no bones of a wolf, and pulls down a red deer without fear or difficulty. I heard my friend set up some most piteous howls (and I assure you the noise was no joke), all occasioned by his fear of passing Puss, who had stationed himself on the stairs.

—SIR WALTER SCOTT,
HINSE OF HINSEFELD

Clicker Training Step 3
Capturing

Newbie clicker folks love *capturing*—marking and reward-ing a behavior a subject offers on his own—and sitting, pawing, stretching, and rolling are perfect natural cat behaviors to use. In addition, you can *shape* or modify a captured behavior in tiny increments: A cat who knows the Gimme Five can learn to have his claws trimmed without fussing! Work on one behav-ior at a time before teaching a new one; don't combine them. All it takes is a couple of two- or three-minute sessions per day.

clicker, 20 or so treats per session

Sit

1. You can teach this while sitting on the couch or standing in front of your cat. Put her on the floor and observe her. Eventually she will decide to sit. As her hindquarters descend to the floor, *click!*—and treat. You have captured a behavior.
2. Nudge her gently to a standing position with your foot if you need to. Every time she starts to sit, click and treat, and repeat. Add the cue, "Sit," just as she is getting ready to do it. Remember, click while the butt is hitting the floor, not after.
3. When you start the second session later that day or the next

one, the cat will have to backtrack a little—but she'll catch on faster the second time around.

4. After about 20 short sessions spread out over, say, 10 days, your cat should sit fairly consistently when you say the cue (but don't expect her to do this in the presence of guests or distractions—this takes a while!).

Gimme Five

1. Wiggle your fist around on the floor in front of your cat. Eventually he will lift a paw or touch your hand. Capture any movement of a paw, even if tentative, with a well-timed *click!*—and treat. Don't ask for a pat at first.

2. Once your cat touches your hand repeatedly for a CT (click and treat), stick your hand out flat on the floor and say, "Gimme five." (Make sure you offer a hand that has not been holding treats, or your cat will sniff instead of pat.) CT a paw movement. It will become a pat with practice. Do not CT for sniffing, or your cat will learn the wrong thing.

3. After you and your cat have nailed this trick, raise your hand a little higher for dramatic effect. Now you are starting to *shape* the behavior.

VARIATION: Want your friends to think your cat can count? Hold your hand above your cat's head and say, "Gimme ten!" Most cats will sit up and place both paws against it.

Puff Muffins

Looking for a nourishing between-meal treat for your cat? Combine the chewy texture of nutritious oatmeal with the salty flavor of chicken broth, and you'll have a snack fit for a king's court at teatime. Puss in Boots would love these.

1$^1/_2$ cups rolled oats
$^1/_2$ cup flour
$^1/_4$ cup corn oil
$^1/_2$ cup chicken broth

1. Preheat the oven to 350°F.
2. Combine all ingredients in a large bowl. Flour your hands and knead until thoroughly mixed.
3. Form the mixture into tiny bite-size muffins and drop onto a greased cookie sheet.

4. Bake for about 15 minutes, or until lightly browned. Store the treats in a sealed container for up to 2 weeks.

Makes about 4–5 cups of treats.

A cat is always on the wrong side of the door.

—Anonymous

The Roaming Cat

by Adlai Stevenson

State of Illinois
Executive Department
Springfield, April 23, 1949

To the Honorable, the Members of the Senate of the 66th General Assembly:

I herewith return, without my approval, Senate Bill No. 93 entitled "An Act to Provide Protection to Insectivorous Birds by Restraining Cats." This is the so-called "Cat Bill." I veto and withhold my approval from this Bill for the following reasons:

It would impose fines on owners or keepers who permitted their cats to run at large off their premises. It would permit any person to capture, or call upon the police to pick up and imprison, cats at large. . . . This legislation has been introduced in the past several sessions of the Legislature, and it has, over the years, been the source of much comment—not all of which has been in a serious vein. . . . I cannot believe there is a widespread public demand for this law or that it could, as a practical matter, be enforced.

Furthermore, I cannot agree that it should be the declared public policy of Illinois that a cat visiting a neighbor's yard or crossing the highway is a public nuisance. It is in the nature of cats to do a certain amount of unescorted roaming. . . . Also consider the owner's dilemma: To escort a cat abroad on a leash is against the nature of the cat, and to permit it to venture forth for exercise unattended into a night of new dangers is against the nature of the owner. Moreover, cats perform useful service, particularly in rural areas, in combating rodents—work they necessarily perform alone and without regard for property lines. . . .

The problem of cat *versus* bird is as old as time. If we attempt to resolve it by legislation who knows but what we may be called upon to take sides as well in the age-old problem of dog *versus* cat, bird *versus* bird, or even bird *versus* worm. In my opinion, the State of Illinois and its local governing bodies already have enough to do without trying to control feline delinquency.

For these reasons, and not because I love birds the less or cats the more, I veto and withhold my approval from Senate Bill No. 93.

Respectfully,
Adlai E. Stevenson, Governor

The Owl and the Pussy-cat

by Edward Lear

The Owl and the Pussy-cat went to sea
  In a beautiful pea-green boat,
They took some honey, and plenty of money,
  Wrapped up in a five-pound note.
The Owl looked up to the stars above,
  And sang to a small guitar,
"O lovely Pussy! O Pussy, my love,
  What a beautiful Pussy you are,
        You are,
        You are!
  What a beautiful Pussy you are!"

Pussy said to the Owl, "You elegant fowl!
  How charmingly sweet you sing!

121

O let us be married! too long have we tarried:
    But what shall we do for a ring!"
They sailed away, for a year and a day,
    To the land where the Bong-tree grows,
And there in a wood a Piggy-wig stood
    With a ring at the end of his nose,
            His nose,
            His nose,
    With a ring at the end of his nose.

"Dear Pig, are you willing to sell for one shilling
    Your ring?" Said the Piggy, "I will."
So they took it away, and were married next day
    By the Turkey who lives on the hill.
They dined on mince, and slices of quince,
    Which they ate with a runcible spoon;
And hand in hand, on the edge of the sand,
    They danced by the light of the moon,
            The moon,
            The moon,
They danced by the light of the moon.

Obstacle Course

While dog agility and equestrian competitions have been in existence for many years, International Cat Agility Tournaments (ICAT) premiered in Albuquerque, New Mexico, in October 2003.

Training animals to complete a course in the correct order relies on a concept called backchaining, in which a number of learned behaviors are strung together. Agility courses comprise pieces of gym equipment for animals. But you don't have to do anything fancy to set up a "cat gym" at home. You can construct most of the elements out of materials such as cardboard boxes, pillows, and plastic cups. Arrange them in a circuit around the room. Use clicker training to help your cat to complete the obstacle course.

Pedestal You might begin your gym workout by asking your cat to jump up and sit on a small stool for a treat. If your cat knows Touch (page 70), you can use this to signal, "Playtime begins!"

Tunnels Indispensable to obstacle-course lovers, these can be bought ready-made or taped together from cardboard cartons.

Weave Course Place four or five upside-down cups or stacking plastic children's cones in a row on the floor and teach your cat to weave back and forth through them by having her follow a toy or the chopstick you use for Touch.

Ramp Build a slight incline up to a small table using a piece of wood, some sturdy cardboard, or a pillow. Secure an old towel around the ramp. The cat can run up the ramp and jump off the other end of the table onto a padded or carpeted surface as part of the course.

Hurdle Incorporate a hop over a hurdle (page 160).

The Cheshire-Cat

by Lewis Carroll

The Cat only grinned when it saw Alice. It looked good-natured, she thought: still it had *very* long claws and a great many teeth, so she felt that it ought to be treated with respect.

"Cheshire-Puss," she began, rather timidly, as she did not at all know whether it would like the name: how-ever, it only grinned a little wider. "Come, it's pleased so far," thought Alice, and she went on. "Would you tell me, please, which way I ought to go from here?"

"That depends a good deal on where you want to get to," said the Cat.

"I don't much care where—" said Alice.

"Then it doesn't matter which way you go," said the Cat.

"—so long as I get *somewhere*," Alice added as an explanation.

"Oh, you're sure to do that," said the Cat, "if you only walk long enough."

Alice felt that this could not be denied, so she tried another question. "What sort of people live about here?"

"In *that* direction," the Cat said, waving its right paw round, "lives a Hatter: and in *that* direction," waving the other paw, "lives a March Hare. Visit either you like: they're both mad."

"But I don't want to go among mad people," Alice remarked.

"Oh, you ca'n't help that," said the Cat: "we're all mad here. I'm mad. You're mad."

"How do you know I'm mad?" said Alice.

"You must be," said the Cat, "or you wouldn't have come here."

Alice didn't think that proved

126

it at all: however, she went on: "And how do you know that you're mad?"

"To begin with," said the Cat, "a dog's not mad. You grant that."

"I suppose so," said Alice.

"Well, then," the Cat went on, "you see a dog growls when it's angry, and wags its tail when it's pleased. Now *I* growl when I'm pleased, and wag my tail when I'm angry. Therefore I'm mad."

"*I* call it purring, not growling," said Alice.

"Call it what you like," said the Cat. "Do you play croquet with the Queen to-day?"

"I should like it very much," said Alice, "but I haven't been invited yet."

"You'll see me there," said the Cat, and vanished.

Alice was not much surprised at this, she was getting so well used to queer things

happening. While she was still looking at the place where it had been, it suddenly appeared again.

"By-the-bye, what became of the baby?" said the Cat. "I'd nearly forgotten to ask."

"It turned into a pig," Alice answered very quietly, just as if the Cat had come back in a natural way.

"I thought it would," said the Cat, and vanished again.

Alice waited a little, half expecting to see it again, but it did not appear, and after a minute or two she walked on in the direction in which the March Hare was said to live. "I've seen hatters before," she said to herself: "the March Hare will be much the most interesting, and perhaps, as this is May, it wo'n't be raving mad— at least not so mad as it was in March." As

128

The Cheshire-Cat

she said this she looked up, and there was the Cat again, sitting on a branch of a tree.

"Did you say 'pig,' or 'fig'?" said the Cat.

"I said 'pig'," replied Alice; "and I wish you wouldn't keep appearing and vanishing so suddenly: you make one quite giddy!"

"All right," said the Cat; and this time it vanished quite slowly, beginning with the end of the tail, and ending with the grin, which remained some time after the rest of it had gone.

"Well! I've often seen a cat without a grin," thought Alice; "but a grin without a cat! It's the most curious thing I ever saw in all my life!"

The cat went here and there
And the moon spun round like a top,
And the nearest kin of the moon,
The creeping cat, looked up.
Black Minnaloushe stared at the moon,
For, wander and wail as he would,
The pure cold light in the sky
Troubled his animal blood.
Minnaloushe runs in the grass
Lifting his delicate feet.
Do you dance, Minnaloushe, do you dance?
When two close kindred meet,
What better than call a dance?
Maybe the moon may learn,
Tired of that courtly fashion,
A new dance turn.
Minnaloushe creeps through the grass
From moonlit place to place,
The sacred moon overhead
Has taken a new phase.
Does Minnaloushe know that his pupils

Will pass from change to change,
And that from round to crescent,
From crescent to round they range?
Minnaloushe creeps through the grass
Alone, important and wise,
And lifts to the changing moon
His changing eyes.

The
Cat
and
the
Moon

by
W. B. Yeats

Magic Box

Great for groups of cats, this simple activity takes advantage of the fact that cats love to sniff and rub any new object in their territory.

cardboard box, a clicker (or use a mouth click), treats or kibble

1. Place a lightweight cardboard carton in the middle of a space. Wait for your cat to notice the box. Make a clicking sound for any interaction, even if your cat just looks at the box from across the room. Then give or toss a treat. If your cat does not show increased interest, toss the box in the air; that often brings furry friends running. Also, consider changing to a tastier treat. Food talks.

2. Each time a cat sniffs, rubs, looks at, meows at, or touches the box in any way, click and treat. He will soon realize that he is being rewarded for having anything to do with the box, and will increase his interaction. If the cat is very active, give a treat after every few clicks.

3. Up the ante. As the cat keeps playing with the box, you might click and treat only when he jumps into or out of the box, or only when he rubs the box. (But don't make it so hard he gets frustrated and walks away!) As you click a particular behavior, the cat will offer that one behavior more often than any other. The cat is being subconsciously conditioned to offer a desired behavior through the rewards you give him. People learn and are socialized in the same way— through positive incentives.

4. Put the box away when you are done with your session; cats eventually become uninterested when it's left out and they stop getting treats.

Cat Outing

One fine sunny day, two robins were lying on their backs, enjoying the sun. A mother cat and her kittens went strolling by. The kittens, as always, were saying how hungry they were and asking what they could have to eat. Their mama, spying the birds, said, "How about some baskin' robins?"

Dick Whittington was a poor boy who lived in the English countryside. He had been orphaned at a young age and had no relatives to speak of. He spent his days scrabbling for a bit to eat, and trying desperately to find a place to sleep each night.

One day, he overheard a man telling his friend about the wondrous city of London. He spoke of how the streets were paved with gold, and how any young man who was willing to work hard would become a gentleman there in no time at all.

"Why, if that's so, I can pry up a bit of cobblestone and be fed for the next month!" Dick thought, "There is nothing for me in this village. I will try my luck in London!" And the very next day he set off on the road

Dick Whittington and his Wonderful Cat

An English Tale

to the city. Moving was very easy for him, as he had no possessions but the shirt on his back and the hope in his heart.

After trekking the long, long road, Dick could just make out the twisted spires and tall buildings of London. And from far away, it did look like a magical place.

But when Dick arrived in the city, he found a very different world than he'd imagined. Instead of gold paving the streets, there were mountains of garbage and waste. Smoke and odor hung in the air, and a million horrible noises fell upon his ears. Dick was afraid, but he had nowhere else to go. So he set about trying to find employment in one of the houses nearby. As his luck would have it, Dick found a job right at his first stop, for that very day a kitchen boy had run away from the Fitzwarren household.

Unfortunately for Dick, the kitchen boy had a good reason to run away: the Fitzwarren kitchen was run by the most mean-hearted cook. All day long she tormented poor Dick, calling him lazy, filthy, and any other horrible insult she could think of. She was never far behind him with a curse on her lips and a frying pan in her hand. She even boarded him in the most rat-plagued room in the house.

"You should be used to rooming with vermin by now," she snorted.

All night long, Dick could hardly sleep due to the small army of mice marching over his bed. But Dick was not ready to give up yet. He began to save up his money, and the first chance he got, he bought a beautiful little tabby cat. Everyone in the house adored her.

"What a sweet little kitten," Fitzwarren's daughter, Sophie, exclaimed, and she spent a great deal of time playing with Dick and his new pet whenever his kitchen duties were done. The cat proved to be a terrific mouser, and Dick's room quickly became the only place in the house that did not host a mouse or two. With his new pet and a pest-free bed, Dick found it easier to bear the cruelties of the horrible cook.

As the years passed, Dick Whittington grew into a strong young man. He worked hard for Mr. Fitzwarren, but no matter what he did, the cook never let up her torrent of abuse. It made life hard for Dick, but he managed to be cheered every time he returned to his dear cat.

The cat, too, had blossomed. She became a large, sleek cat who kept the house free of all kinds of mice and vermin. She was so good at her job that the family sometimes good-naturedly grumbled about oversleeping.

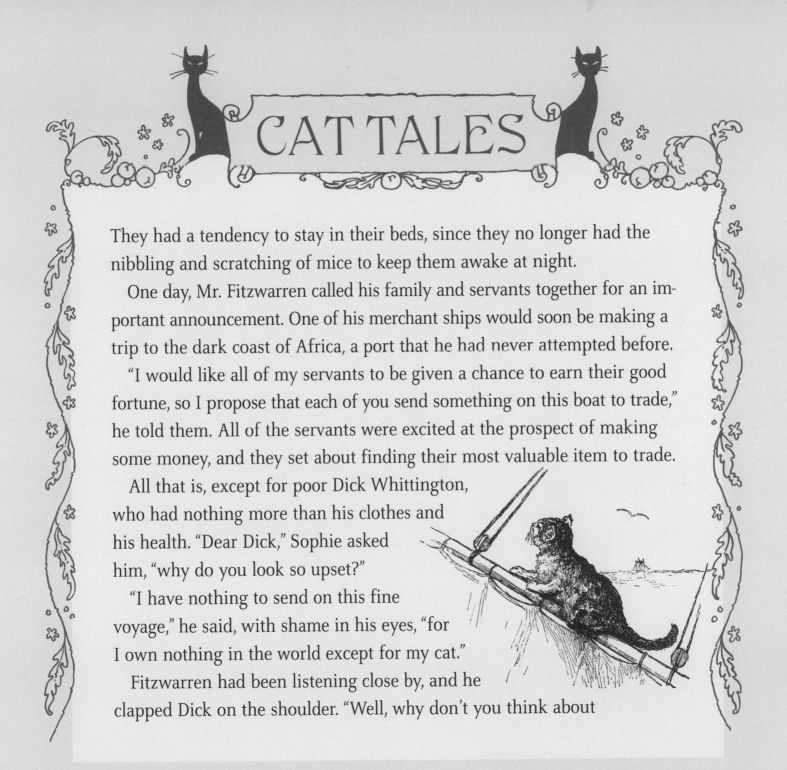

They had a tendency to stay in their beds, since they no longer had the nibbling and scratching of mice to keep them awake at night.

One day, Mr. Fitzwarren called his family and servants together for an important announcement. One of his merchant ships would soon be making a trip to the dark coast of Africa, a port that he had never attempted before.

"I would like all of my servants to be given a chance to earn their good fortune, so I propose that each of you send something on this boat to trade," he told them. All of the servants were excited at the prospect of making some money, and they set about finding their most valuable item to trade.

All that is, except for poor Dick Whittington, who had nothing more than his clothes and his health. "Dear Dick," Sophie asked him, "why do you look so upset?"

"I have nothing to send on this fine voyage," he said, with shame in his eyes, "for I own nothing in the world except for my cat."

Fitzwarren had been listening close by, and he clapped Dick on the shoulder. "Well, why don't you think about

CAT TALES

sending along your cat? We all know that she is a fine mouser. I'm certain she will keep the ship clear of any pests that may want to get on board."

Dick was reluctant to let his little cat go, as she was his dearest friend in the world, but he did want to make something of himself. Finally, he gave his consent to send her on the journey.

After his cat was gone, Dick was more miserable than ever. The cook seemed crueler than she had ever been before, and even Sophie could not cheer him up. After an especially bad assault from the cook one evening, Dick decided he had had enough of the Fitzwarren household and ran away. He was halfway down the street, when he suddenly heard the bells of London ringing. Now, he had heard them ring on more times than he could think of, but for some reason, this time they seemed to be saying, "Turn again, Whittington, Lord Mayor of London!"

"I don't believe my ears!" Dick thought, "Could I really be Lord Mayor one day?" He didn't think that dream would ever come true, but he did resolve to turn back and try his luck again at the Fitzwarren household.

Months passed, and things stayed relatively the same, until one day, Sophie came running into the kitchen. "Quick, Father sent me to fetch

CAT TALES

you, Dick! He said he has a wonderful surprise for you at the ships!" He followed her as quickly as lightning to the docks, where he saw Fitzwarren overseeing the unloading of cargo. Almost before he knew it, a tiny orange shape darted over the deck and leapt into his arms! It was his beautiful cat, alive and purring next to his heart!

"This is the most wonderful surprise ever!" Dick shouted, but Fitzwarren interrupted his reunion. "I am glad to see you so happy, Dick, but she's not the surprise I was talking about!" He gave a signal and barrel after barrel of gold coins were rolled out and placed in front of Dick.

"To whom do these riches belong ?" Dick whispered in awe.

"Why," replied Fitzwarren, "to you, my son."

He explained that when the captain and crew arrived in Africa, they were met by a nobleman and his wife and invited to dinner. But when they sat down at the meal, they were barely able to salvage a crumb. You see, mice had completely overrun their household, and due to a strange sickness that had swept through the village, they had no cats to deter them! The captain immediately thought of Dick's cat, and brought her to the house, where she proceeded to wreak havoc on the mouse population.

CAT TALES

The noble couple was so taken by her that they let her sleep on a pillow of silk, and rewarded her with tubs of cream to drink. Dick's cat settled down, and even had a litter of kittens that turned out to be just as excellent at hunting mice as their mother was. When the time came to leave, the kittens became the royal pets of the household, and the couple totaled up the entire sum of the cargo of the ship, and then doubled it as payment for what Dick's cat had done!

And so Dick got his cat back and became very wealthy in the process. He used his money towards an education and built his own fine merchant business. He became a very successful gentleman in his time, and eventually asked for the hand of Sophie Fitzwarren in marriage. The happy couple lived at the house for a great many years, and Dick was voted Lord Mayor of London, not once, but twice!

Dick Whittington never forgot how he owed his fortune to one small cat. And Dick's cat, in turn, repaid his love by keeping his house completely free of mice until the end of her days.

Lamb and Rice Delight

Lamb and rice are both popular cat food ingredients. Here's a healthy snack that appeals to your feline's fondness for protein and fat, with a little extra "zing" thrown in.

4 ounces ground lamb
$1/4$ cup cooked rice
2 tablespoons cornmeal
1 egg
1 teaspoon catnip
dash of salt

1. Preheat the broiler to 425°F. Combine all the ingredients and knead the mixture into a ball.
2. Place on a greased cookie sheet and flatten to a thickness of about 1/2 inch.
3. Broil for 4 minutes on each side, or until crisp. Let it cool for 30 minutes.
4. Cut into small treat-size pieces. These will keep for up to a week in a sealed container in the refrigerator.

Makes about 6 dozen treats.

She sights a Bird—she chuckles—
She flattens—then she crawls—
She runs without the look of feet—
Her eyes increase to Balls—

Her Jaws stir—twitching—hungry—
Her Teeth can hardly stand—
She leaps, but Robin leaped the first—
Ah, Pussy, of the Sand,

The Hopes so juicy ripening—
You almost bathed your Tongue—
When Bliss disclosed a hundred Toes—
And fled with every one—

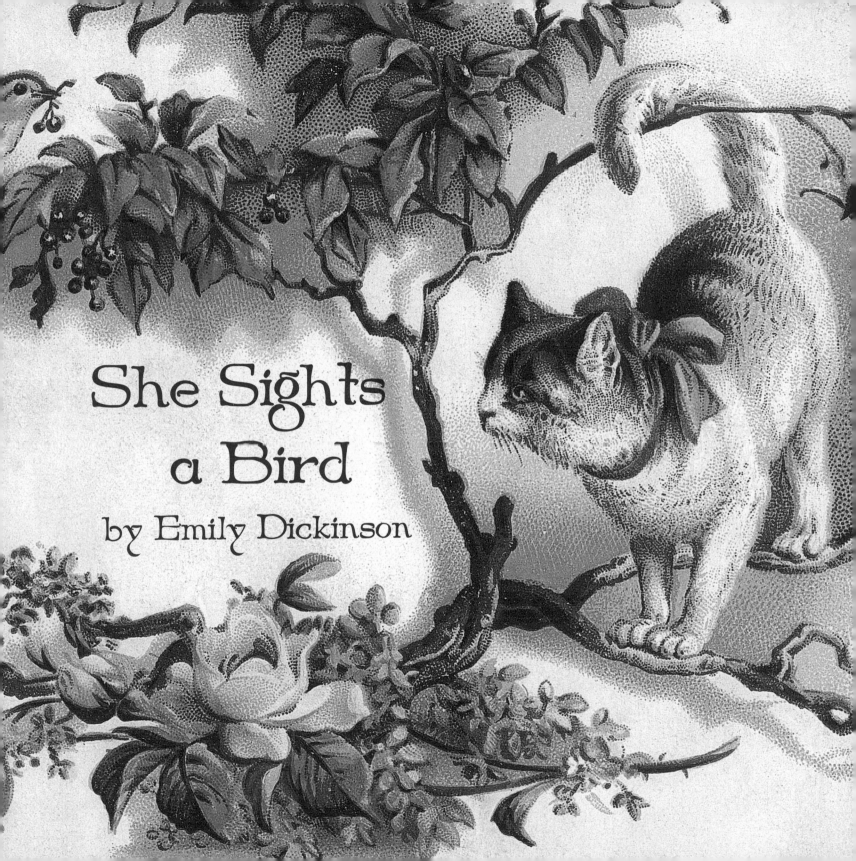

She Sights a Bird

by Emily Dickinson

The cat loves fish... but does not like to wet her paws.

— ENGLISH PROVERB

Cat in the Rain
by Ernest Hemingway

There were only two Americans stopping at the hotel. They did not know any of the people they passed on the stairs on their way to and from their room. Their room was on the second floor facing the sea. It also faced the public garden and the war monument. There were big palms and green benches in the public garden. In the good weather there was always an artist with his easel. Artists liked the way the palms grew and the bright colors of the hotels facing the gardens and the sea. Italians came from a long way off to look up at the war monument. It was made of bronze and glistened in the rain. It was raining. The rain dripped from the palm trees. Water stood in pools on the gravel paths. The sea broke in a long line in the rain and slipped back down the beach to come up and break again in a long line in the rain. The motor cars were gone from the square by the war monument. Across the square in the doorway of the café a waiter stood looking out at the empty square.

The American wife stood at the window looking out. Outside right under their window a cat was crouched under one of the dripping green tables. The cat was trying to make herself so compact that she would not be dripped on.

"I'm going down and get that kitty," the American wife said.

"I'll do it," her husband offered from the bed.

"No, I'll get it. The poor kitty out trying to keep dry under a table."

The husband went on reading, lying propped up with the two pillows at the foot of the bed.

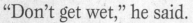

Cat in the Rain

"Don't get wet," he said.

The wife went downstairs and the hotel owner stood up and bowed to her as she passed the office. His desk was at the far end of the office. He was an old man and very tall.

"Il poive," the wife said. She liked the hotel-keeper.

"Si, si, Signora, brutto tempo. It's very bad weather."

He stood behind his desk in the far end of the dim room. The wife liked him. She liked the deadly serious way he received any complaints. She liked his dignity. She liked the way he wanted to serve her. She liked the way he felt about being a hotel-keeper. She liked his old, heavy face and big hands.

Liking him she opened the door and looked out. It was raining harder. A man in a rubber cape was crossing the empty square to the café. The cat would be around to the right. Perhaps she could go along under the eaves. As she stood in the doorway an umbrella opened behind her. It was the maid who looked after their room.

"You must not get wet," she smiled, speaking Italian. Of course, the hotel-keeper had sent her.

With the maid holding the umbrella over her, she walked along the gravel path until she was under their window. The table was there, washed bright green in the rain, but the cat was gone. She was suddenly disappointed. The maid looked up at her.

"Ha perduto qualque cosa, Signora?"

"There was a cat," said the American girl.

"A cat?"

"Si, il gatto."

"A cat?" the maid laughed. "A cat in the rain?"

"Yes," she said, "under the table." Then, "Oh, I wanted it so much. I wanted a kitty."

154

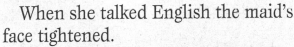

When she talked English the maid's face tightened.

"Come, Signora," she said. "We must get back inside. You will be wet."

"I suppose so," said the American girl.

They went back along the gravel path and passed in the door. The maid stayed outside to close the umbrella. As the American girl passed the office, the padrone bowed from his desk. Something felt very small and tight inside the girl. The padrone made her feel very small and at the same time really important. She had a momentary feeling of being of supreme importance. She went on up the stairs. She opened the door of the room. George was on the bed, reading.

"Did you get the cat?" he asked, putting the book down.

"It was gone."

"Wonder where it went to," he said, resting his eyes from reading.

She sat down on the bed.

"I wanted it so much," she said. "I don't know why I wanted it so much. I wanted that poor kitty. It isn't any fun to be a poor kitty out in the rain."

George was reading again.

She went over and sat in front of the mirror of the dressing table looking at herself with the hand glass. She studied her profile, first one side and then the other. Then she studied the back of her head and her neck.

"Don't you think it would be a good idea if I let my hair grow

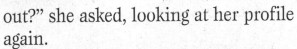

Cat in the Rain

out?" she asked, looking at her profile again.

George looked up and saw the back of her neck, clipped close like a boy's.

"I like it the way it is."

"I get so tired of it," she said. "I get so tired of looking like a boy."

George shifted his position in the bed. He hadn't looked away from her since she started to speak.

"You look pretty darn nice," he said.

She laid the mirror down on the dresser and went over to the window and looked out. It was getting dark.

"I want to pull my hair back tight and smooth and make a big knot at the back that I can feel," she said. "I want to have a kitty to sit on my lap and purr when I stroke her."

"Yeah?" George said from the bed.

"And I want to eat at a table with my own silver and I want candles. And I want it to be spring and I want to brush my hair out in front of a mirror and I want a kitty and I want some new clothes."

"Oh, shut up and get something to read," George said. He was reading again.

His wife was looking out of the window. It was quite dark now and still raining in the palm trees.

"Anyway, I want a cat," she said, "I want a cat. I want a cat now. If I can't have long hair or any fun, I can have a cat."

George was not listening. He was reading his book. His wife looked out of the window where the light had come on in the square.

Someone knocked at the door.

"Avanti," George said. He looked up from his book.

In the doorway stood the maid. She held a big tortoise-shell cat pressed tight against her and swung down against her body.

"Excuse me," she said, "the padrone asked me to bring this for the Signora."

157

Easy Toys for Kitty

Your cat doesn't care whether you spend a lot of money on toys. The key to capturing a cat's interest is a toy that is light in weight. Heavy toys such as the rubber Kongs used for dog play don't work with cats. Beadbags are lighter than beanbags.

Beadbag

strong cotton flannel, chamois, or felt (4" x 8" or smaller); needle and thread (or sewing machine); lightweight hollow plastic beads from a hobby supply store

1. Fold the fabric in half the short way and stitch, using fine stitches or a fine setting on your sewing machine, around three edges, leaving a 1-inch opening. Make sure the stitching is secure enough that the cat can't pull out any thread.

2. Turn the bag right-side out and fill it with beads. Don't overfill or make it heavy. For added intrigue, put in a piece of crinkly cellophane.
3. Sew the opening tightly shut, and toss! Cats like the feel of the extra-soft fabric.

Kitty Kong

toilet paper roll, a small amount of peanut butter

1. If your cat isn't crazy about peanut butter, you can substitute processed cheese food, like Cheez Whiz. Smear a small amount of peanut butter or cheese inside the toilet paper tube (don't overdo it)—just enough so that your pet can smell it or get a tiny taste.
2. Toss the tube and watch the action!

158

Clicker Training Step 4
Luring

Expert clicker trainers don't like it when an animal trainer leads a pet through a series of performances with a piece of food in front of his face—that's not really training, after all. Nevertheless, a little luring—leading the cat by dangling a desired object in front of him—can be helpful at the very beginning, when you just need to get the behavior. Hurdling, a great exercise for a flabby tabby, can be taught in no time, and is extremely self-reinforcing (fun).

Hurdling
yardstick, broom, or dowel; two stacks of books;
chopstick (optional); clicker; treats

1. Set this up for success, meaning that you erect the hurdle in a hallway or bathroom so that Kitty can't walk around it, and make it low enough so she doesn't limbo. Place a yardstick, broom, or dowel on two stacks of books.
2. Simply make a motion with the chopstick or your hand and say "Over." The cat may step over the stick at first—that's okay.
3. CT (click and treat) the moment all four feet touch the floor on the other side.

Sit Pretty

clicker, treats, chopstick (optional)

1. Invite the cat to sit. CT (click and treat).
2. Ask your cat to sit up by wiggling your fingers above and in front of her head; lure with a treat if you can't get her up. Alternatively, if she is good with the Touch, you can lure with the chopstick.
3. With the other hand, click as she is reaching the top of her ascent, and before she bats at you. Try not to click as she is on her way down, or you will be teaching her to bob. The food lure may be necessary to teach her to start holding the position. (Don't try to make her hold it too long.) Keep CT'ing those reps!
4. Once she starts to get it, add the cue, "Sit pretty."

CAT TALES

Once upon a time there was a fierce and courageous samurai, who was an expert with weapons. His skill with the sword was known throughout the land, and people said that no man or woman could defeat him.

One afternoon as the samurai was placing a bit of fish on the table for his meal, a rat crept stealthily from behind the counter and snatched it away. The samurai saw only its long, oily tail as it dashed into its hiding place.

"Why should I, the greatest samurai in the land, have to share my house

The Samurai's Dilemma

A Japanese Folktale

with such filthy vermin?" he asked himself. The samurai resolved to rid his house of the rat by any means possible. And so his battle began.

On the first day of battle, the samurai hid himself in a corner and waited for the rat. When he saw his enemy at last, the samurai sprang at the furry menace with sword upraised, but the rat moved like lightning and was back to his hole before the sword was even brought down.

Next, the samurai baited traps with delicious morsels and waited for the rat to fall for his trick, but again the wily rat managed to avoid the traps and succeeded in stealing the samurai's dinner. With only a few morsels left on the table, the samurai went to bed hungry for a second night.

On the second day, the samurai comforted himself saying, "I am a very rich man thanks to my many battles. I shall easily buy more food later, but first I must finish this pest," and with that he descended into the village.

At the local dojo, where young warriors practiced their arts, the samurai humbled himself and asked for the help of the master.

"I am looking for a warrior so strong and brave, the rat will have no chance of escape," he declared.

"Look no further," the master, said, motioning to a large tabby. His left ear was half-bitten off and he had a long scar over one of his

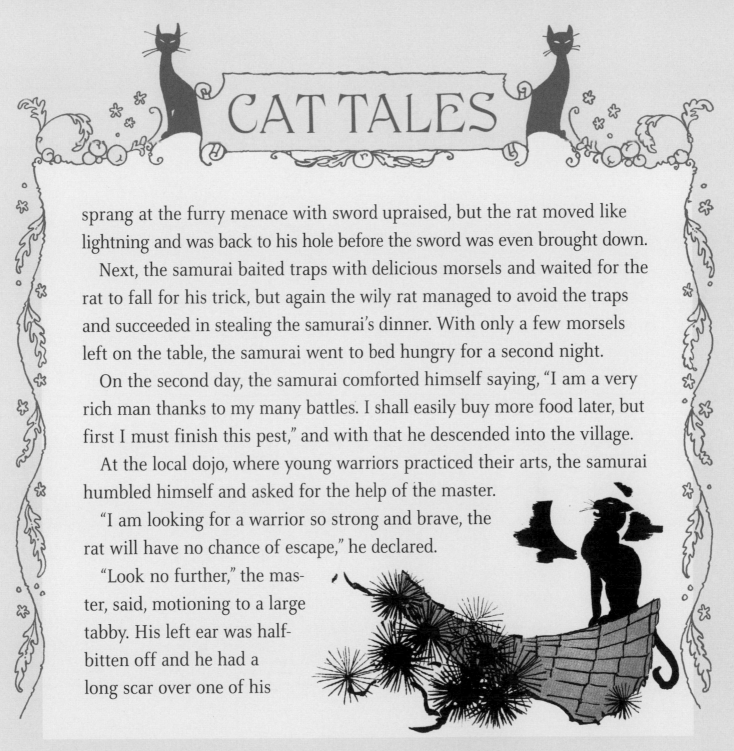

eyes. "This cat has fought many battles, and he will live to fight many more!"

The samurai was pleased with such an experienced cat and immediately took him back to the house.

As soon as the rat saw the tabby, he stood absolutely still and stared at the feline warrior. The cat glared back, with a piercing gaze that would set paper aflame. The face-off continued for several breathless moments until, to the samurai's amazement, the cat suddenly dropped his eyes in defeat and ran from the house!

The samurai knew then that this was no ordinary rat. He grabbed his sack of coins to throw at the rat, only to discover that it was surprisingly light. Upon further inspection, the samurai found the rat had chewed a whole in the pouch and stolen the coins!

The samurai went to sleep, hungry and poor.

On the third day, the samurai comforted himself saying, "I am a man with many beautiful things. I shall easily sell my silks and art for money, but first I must finish this pest," and with that he descended into the village.

He went to the local wise man and explained his problem.

"I know a magical cat so swift that she appears like a shadow and

CAT TALES

CAT TALES

attacks like smoke. The rat will never even see his enemy until he is clenched between her jaws!" the wise man explained, as he showed the samurai a cat that was black as night. When the cat closed her eyes, she seemed to disappear altogether!

"This will do nicely," the samurai agreed, and took the magical cat to meet her adversary.

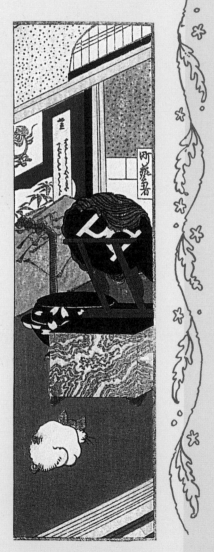

As soon as the cat entered the house, she shut her eyes and dissolved into the shadows deep in the corner of the room. The rat, appearing oblivious, meandered out to nibble on the last piece of fruit the samurai had.

Suddenly, the cat materialized and leapt for the rat— only to grab empty space! The rat had deftly jumped from the table before the cat could land. Like quick-silver, the rat swiftly turned and bit his opponent's tail.

The cat let out a piercing yowl and ran from the samurai's house, never to return.

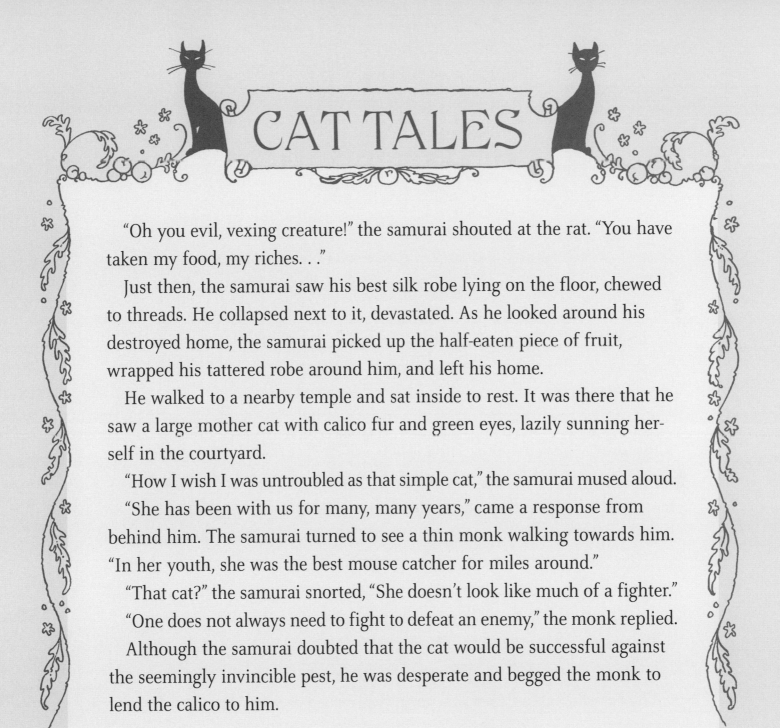

CAT TALES

"Oh you evil, vexing creature!" the samurai shouted at the rat. "You have taken my food, my riches. . ."

Just then, the samurai saw his best silk robe lying on the floor, chewed to threads. He collapsed next to it, devastated. As he looked around his destroyed home, the samurai picked up the half-eaten piece of fruit, wrapped his tattered robe around him, and left his home.

He walked to a nearby temple and sat inside to rest. It was there that he saw a large mother cat with calico fur and green eyes, lazily sunning herself in the courtyard.

"How I wish I was untroubled as that simple cat," the samurai mused aloud.

"She has been with us for many, many years," came a response from behind him. The samurai turned to see a thin monk walking towards him. "In her youth, she was the best mouse catcher for miles around."

"That cat?" the samurai snorted, "She doesn't look like much of a fighter."

"One does not always need to fight to defeat an enemy," the monk replied.

Although the samurai doubted that the cat would be successful against the seemingly invincible pest, he was desperate and begged the monk to lend the calico to him.

CAT TALES

Upon returning to his house with the cat, the samurai was infuriated to see how the rat had destroyed his precious books and paintings.

"That's it, rat!" he exclaimed. But when he put the cat down, she merely yawned, looked around, and then settled into the sunniest part of the room. The samurai looked at his house in shambles, threw up his hands, and retired to his bedroom in defeat. It seemed that the rat was victorious.

For the next few days, the cat did little else but snooze on one of the samurai's prayer cushions. The rat now had the run of the household, and grew bolder with each passing moment. No place was safe from his sharp teeth and scurrying feet, and because the cat put up no opposition, the rat began to feel he was recognized as the superior in the household.

"That cat is little more than a servant to me," thought the rat haughtily as he passed her to retrieve a large piece of bread.

The bread was so heavy, that the rat decided he shouldn't have to deal with carrying it on his own.

"Hey, Puss," he called, "get over here and help me with this!"

The cat opened her eyes, got up, and stretched slowly. She walked over

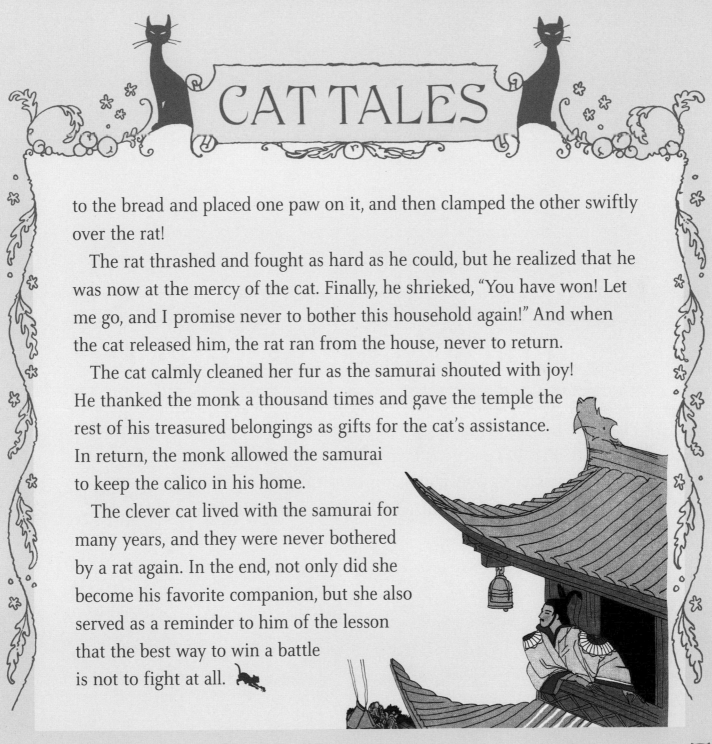

to the bread and placed one paw on it, and then clamped the other swiftly over the rat!

The rat thrashed and fought as hard as he could, but he realized that he was now at the mercy of the cat. Finally, he shrieked, "You have won! Let me go, and I promise never to bother this household again!" And when the cat released him, the rat ran from the house, never to return.

The cat calmly cleaned her fur as the samurai shouted with joy! He thanked the monk a thousand times and gave the temple the rest of his treasured belongings as gifts for the cat's assistance. In return, the monk allowed the samurai to keep the calico in his home.

The clever cat lived with the samurai for many years, and they were never bothered by a rat again. In the end, not only did she become his favorite companion, but she also served as a reminder to him of the lesson that the best way to win a battle is not to fight at all.

Kittens believe that all nature is occupied with their diversion.

—Augustin-Paradis de Moncrif

Kibble Dribble

Playing games brings you and your cat closer together. You'll be impressed by your cat's intelligence and his desire to please you (after all, you are his food source!) once he realizes that you want to interact with him on his terms. Kibble Dribble is great fun for kids and satisfies a cat's natural urge to catch and play with prey—just the ticket for a housebound puss who never gets to practice his hunting skills. Most cats use a double-pawed style, but we know one cat who likes to catch and pick up kibble between the toes of one foot. She either eats it out of her paw or sidearms it into the air and chases it!

hard, smooth flooring surface for "bowling" (such as in a kitchen or bathroom), small-size kibble (not treats), a cat ready for action

1. Take up your cat's regular food and water from his feeding area if it's close by.
2. Bowl or bounce a couple of pieces of kibble hard past your cat and watch him try to block. He may even whack them right back at you.
3. If he starts out by eating the kibble right away, keep bowling; he'll catch on, and will spend time "dribbling" it before snacking. Many cats go wild over this, spinning in circles, leaping, and dancing over their "prey."

The Kittens' Quartet

by Carrie Jacobs-Bond

O see, O see the little birds,
  The little birds, the little birds,
O see, O see the little birds,
  All singing in the tree.
All singing in the tree, the tree,
  All singing in the tree;
I suppose they belong to somebody else,
  But I whish they belonged to me.

Playtime Safety

When choosing or making a pet toy, behaviorists recommend that you not give anything to your cat that you wouldn't give to a three-year-old. This means no harmful parts, such as glitter, tinsel, buttons, or small, unconcealed jingle bells that could come off and be accidentally swallowed. String, lengths of yarn, thread, fishing line, and rubber bands can be swallowed whole, causing intestinal obstruction. The end of a string can be swallowed while the other end gets caught around kitty's tongue. If you see string, thread, or yarn hanging out of your cat's mouth, do not pull on it; it can cut her internally. Rush her to your veterinarian. Elastic cords and feathers, too, are often chewed through; these toys are meant for supervised, interactive use only, and should be put away when playtime's over. Conversely, say vets, there is no harm done if a healthy cat shreds up and happens to eat some pieces of a paper bag.

Cats often like to hide out in plastic bags, but if they get their head stuck in a handle, they might panic, causing choking or suffocating.

According to the ASPCA, you should never use your hands or fingers as play objects with kittens. This type of rough play may cause biting and scratching behaviors to develop as your kitten matures.

Clicker Training Step 5
Shaping

You've already tried a little shaping—modifying a behavior in tiny increments—with the Gimme Ten. Zen Kitty is for the clicker-wise cat who has learned the Gimme Five (page 113), and will test your pet's understanding of the clicker game.

Cats *adore* Pick It Up—especially kittens, who love to put things in their mouths. It's also a challenging way to learn more about how to shape behaviors.

As you continue to practice for a few minutes every day, your cat will begin to offer desirable behaviors more frequently, and will spend less time on destructive projects. After she learns this trick, she may start bringing you all manner of items from around the house.

clicker, treats, and props as required below

Pick It Up

1. Place a lightweight toy or foam ball, reserved for training only, in front of the cat. CT as you see the jaw start to move. Wiggle it around if he doesn't bite it.
2. "Accidentally" bump it into his mouth. CT! If the jaw starts

to open, click fast, and treat.
Repeat. CT for contact, biting,
and finally pickups, and add
the verbal cue, "Pick it up."

Zen Kitty

1. This is for the clicker-wise cat
   who has learned the Gimme
   Five. Present him with two fists:
   one empty, one with a treat inside.
   He will have a tendency to go for the one
   with the treat, but wiggle the empty one. If
   he gets so frustrated he walks away, try
   withdrawing the hand with the treat and
   simply CT'ing him a few times for patting an
   empty fist.
2. Start over with the two fists. As soon as he pats
   the empty fist, CT, open the other hand, and let
   him retrieve the delicious treasure inside. Repeat
   the Zen experience.

The White and Black Dynasties

by Théophile Gautier

– i –

To gain the friendship of a cat is not an easy thing. It is a philosophic, well-regulated, tranquil animal, a creature of habit and a lover of order and cleanliness. It does not give its affections indiscriminately. It will consent to be your friend if you are worthy of the honor, but it will not be your slave. With all its affection, it preserves its freedom of judgment, and it will not do anything for you which it considers unreasonable; but once it has given its love, what absolute confidence, what fidelity of affection! It will make itself the companion of your hours of work, of loneliness, or of sadness. It will lie the whole evening on your knee, purring and happy in your society, and leaving the company of creatures of its own kind to be with you. In vain the sound of caterwauling reverberates from the house-tops, inviting it to one of those cats' evening parties where essence of red-herring takes the place of tea. It will not be tempted, but continues to keep its vigil with you. If you put it down it climbs up again quickly, with a sort of crooning noise, which is like a gentle reproach. Sometimes, when seated in front of you, it gazes at you with such soft, melting eyes, such a human and caressing look, that you are almost awed, for it seems impossible that reason can be absent from it.

– i i –

I called her Seraphita, in memory of Balzac's Swedenborgian

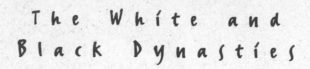

The White and Black Dynasties

romance. The heroine of that wonderful story, when she climbed the snow peaks of the Falberg with Minna, never shone with a more pure white radiance. Seraphita had a dreamy and pensive character. She would lie motionless on a cushion for hours, not asleep, but with eyes fixed in rapt attention on

scenes invisible to ordinary mortals. Caresses were agreeable to her, but she responded to them with great reserve, and only to those of people whom she favored with her esteem, which it was not easy to gain. She liked luxury, and it was always in the newest armchair or on the piece of furniture best calculated to show off her swan-like beauty, that she was to be found. Her toilette took an immense time. She would carefully smooth her entire coat every morning, and wash her face with her paw, and every hair on her body shone like new silver when brushed by her pink tongue. If anyone touched her she would immediately efface all traces of the contact, for she could not endure being ruffled. Her elegance and distinction gave one an idea of aristocratic birth, and among her own kind she must have been at least a duchess. She had a passion for scents. She would plunge her

184

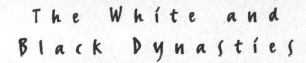

nose into bouquets, and nibble a perfumed handkerchief with little paroxysms of delight. She would walk about on the dressing-table sniffling the stoppers of the scent-bottles, and she would have loved to use the violet powder if she had been allowed.

Such was Seraphita, and ncvcr was a cat more worthy of a poetic name.

— i i i —

Don Pierrot, like all animals which are spoilt and made much of, developed a charming amiability of character. He shared the life of the household with all the pleasure which cats find in the intimacy of the domestic hearth. Seated in his usual place near the fire, he really appeared to understand what was being said, and to take an interest in it. His eyes followed the speakers, and from time to time he would utter little sounds, as though he too wanted to make remarks and give his opinion on literature, which was our usual topic of conversation. He was very fond of books, and when he found one open on a table he would lie on it, look at the page attentively, and turn over the leaves with his paw; then he would end by going to sleep, for all the world as if he were reading a fashionable novel.

Directly I took up a pen he would jump on my writing-desk and with deep attention watch the steel nib tracing black spider-

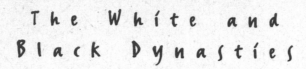

legs on the expanse of white paper, and his head would turn each time I began a new line. Sometimes he tried to take part in the work, and would attempt to pull the pen out of my hand, no doubt in order to write himself, for he was an aesthetic cat, like Hoffman's Murr, and I strongly suspect him of having scribbled his memoirs at night on some house-top by the light of his phosphorescent eyes. Unfortunately these lucubrations have been lost.

Don Pierrot never went to bed until I came in. He waited for me inside the door, and as I entered the hall he would rub himself against my legs and arch his back, purring joyfully all the time. Then he proceeded to walk in front of me like a page, and if I had asked him, he would certainly have carried the candle for me. In this fashion he escorted me to my room and waited while I undressed; then he would jump on the bed, put his paws round my neck, rub noses with me, and lick me with his rasping little pink tongue, while giving vent to soft inarticulate cries, which clearly expressed how pleased he was to see me again. Then when his transports of affection had subsided, and the hour for repose had come, he would balance himself on the rail of the bedstead and sleep there like a bird perched on a bough. When I woke in the morning he would come and lie near me until it was time to get up. Twelve o'clock was the hour at

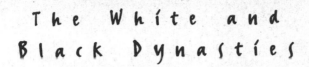
which I was supposed to come in. On this subject Pierrot had all the notions of a concierge.

At that time we had instituted little evening gatherings among a few friends, and had formed a small society, which we called the Four Candles Club, the room in which we met being, as it happened, lit by four candles in silver candlesticks, which were placed at the corners of the table.

Sometimes the conversation became so lively that I forgot the time, at the risk of finding, like Cinderella, my carriage turned into a pumpkin and my coachman into a rat.

Pierrot waited for me several times until two o'clock in the morning, but in the end my conduct displeased him, and he went to bed without me. This mute protest against my innocent dissipation touched me so much that ever after I came home regularly at midnight. But it was a long time before Pierrot forgave

me. He wanted to be sure that it was not a sham repentance; but when he was convinced of the sincerity of my conversion, he deigned to take me into favor again, and he resumed his nightly post in the entrance-hall.

– i v –

Enjolras was by far the handsomest of his family. He was remarkable for his great leonine head and big ruff, his powerful shoulders, long back and splendid feathery tail. There was something theatrical about him, and he seemed to be always posing like a popular actor who knows he is being admired. His movements were slow, undulating and majestic. He put each foot down with as much circumspection as if he were walking on a table covered with Chinese bric-à-brac or Venetian glass. As to his character, he was by no means a stoic, and he showed a love of eating which that virtuous and sober

The White and Black Dynasties

young man, his namesake, would certainly have disapproved. Enjolras would undoubtedly have said to him, like the angel to Swedenborg: "You eat too much."

I humored this gluttony, which was as amusing as a gastronomic monkey's, and Enjolras attained a size and weight seldom reached by the domestic cat. It occurred to me to have him shaved poodle-fashion, so as to give the finishing touch to his resemblance to a lion.

We left him his mane and a big tuft at the end of his tail, and I would not swear that we did not give him mutton-chop whiskers on his haunches like those Munito wore. Thus tricked out, it must be confessed he was much more like a Japanese monster than an African lion. Never was a more fantastic whim carved out of a living animal.

His shaven skin took odd blue tints, which contrasted strangely with his black mane.

— v —

The cat named after the interesting Eponine was more delicate and slender than her brothers. Her nose was rather long, and her eyes slightly oblique, and green as those of Pallas Athene, to whom Homer always applied the epithet of γλαυχωπιζ. Her nose was of velvety black, with the grain of a fine Périgord truffle; her whiskers were in a perpetual state of agitation, all of which gave her a peculiarly expressive countenance. Her superb black coat was always in motion, and was watered and shot with shadowy markings. Never was there a more sensitive, nervous, electric animal. If one stroked her two or three times in the dark, blue sparks would fly crackling out of her fur.

Eponine attached herself particularly to me, like the Eponine of the novel to Marius, but I, being less taken up with Cosette than that handsome young man, could

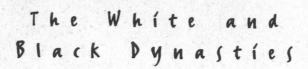

accept the affection of this gentle and devoted cat, who still shares the pleasure of my suburban retreat and is the inseparable companion of my hours of work.

She comes running up when she hears the front-door bell, receives the visitors, conducts them to the drawing-room, talks to them—yes, talks to them—with little chirruping sounds, that do not in the least resemble the language cats use in talking to their own kind, but which simulate the articulate speech of man. What does she say? She says in the clearest way, "Will you be good enough to wait till monsieur comes down? Please look at the pictures, or chat with me in the meantime, if that will amuse you." Then when I come in she discreetly retires to an armchair or a corner of the piano, like a well-bred animal who knows what is correct in good society. Pretty little Eponine gave so many proofs of intelligence, good disposition and sociability, that by common consent she was raised to the dignity of a *person*, for it was quite evident that she was possessed of higher reasoning power than mere instinct. This dignity conferred on her the privilege of eating at table like a person instead of out of a saucer in a corner of the room like an animal.

So Eponine had a chair next to me at breakfast and dinner, but on account of her small size she was allowed to rest her two front paws on the edge of the table. Her place was laid, without spoon or fork, but she had her glass. She went right through dinner dish by dish, from soup to dessert, waiting for her turn to be helped, and behaving with

190

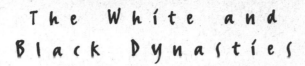

such propriety and nice manners as one would like to see in many children. She made her appearance at the first sound of the bell, and on going into the dining-room one found her already in her place, sitting up in her chair with her paws resting on the edge of the table-cloth, and seeming to offer you her little face to kiss, like a well-brought-up little girl who is affectionately polite towards her parents and elders.

As one finds flaws in diamonds, spots on the sun, and shadows on perfection itself, so Eponine, it must be confessed, had a passion for fish. She shared this in common with all other cats. Contrary to the Latin proverb,

"Catus amat pisces, sed non vult tingere plantas,"

she would willingly have dipped her paw into the water if by so doing she could have pulled out a trout or a young carp. She became nearly frantic over fish, and, like a child who is filled with the expectation of dessert, she sometimes rebelled at her soup when she knew (from previous investigations in the kitchen) that fish was coming. When this happened she was not helped, and I would say to her coldly: "Mademoiselle, a person who is not hungry for soup cannot be hungry for fish," and the dish would be pitilessly carried away from under her nose. Convinced that matters were serious, greedy Eponine would swallow her soup in all haste, down to the last drop, polishing off the last crumb of bread or bit of macaroni, and would then turn round and look at me with pride, like someone who has conscientiously done his duty. She was then given her portion, which she consumed with great satisfaction, and after tasting of every dish in turn, she would finish up by drinking a third of a glass of water.

I value in the cat the independent and almost ungrateful spirit which prevents her from attaching herself to any one, the indifference with which she passes from the salon to the housetop. When we caress her, she stretches herself and arches her back responsively; but this is because she feels an agreeable sensation, not because she takes a silly satisfaction, like the dog, in faithfully loving a thankless master. The cat lives alone, has no need of society, obeys only when she pleases, pretends to sleep that she may see the more clearly, and scratches everything on which she can lay her paw.

—CHATEAUBRIAND, *AN APPRECIATION*

The touch of a hand is warm, soothing, and relaxing. Working animals such as police and assistance dogs, performing animals, and therapy pets, who are subjected to daily stresses, often benefit from regular therapeutic rubdowns. Why not your house cat, too? Once you have developed a bond with your cat through massage, you may even be able to tell when he isn't feeling well.

TAKE YOUR CUES FROM YOUR CAT Massage therapists who have transferred their knowledge to working with cats say the secret is: Don't massage areas that the cat doesn't want touched. Let your cat advise you of what she likes and doesn't like. Next time your "belly cat" plunges in front of you, take a moment to honor her invitation. Begin at her chest and stroke in little circles, moving lightly downward. When your little sidestroker solicits you by "swimming" toward you on the carpet, think how he might appreciate a deep, gentle shoulder rub with your thumbs. And your "bowing cat" who asks you to "thump her rump" might enjoy a vigorous friction backrub to work the kinks out. Take a few moments to try massage on a regular basis.

USE YOUR HANDS AS GROOMING TOOLS Dampening your palms will allow you to get rid of shed fur that is trapped in the coat and that the cat would ingest through licking. Stroke in all directions with the flats of your hands. Then run through the fur one more time, checking the skin with your fingertips for lesions, ticks, or bites.

Massaging Your Cat

START WITH THE SPINE Work your thumbs and fingers in a circular pattern along the sides of the backbone from neck to tail, never losing touch with the skin. Move to the sides, then along the hips and back legs. Return to the shoulders.

PAY ATTENTION TO FAVORITE AREAS There is no end to the annals of weird things cats like—we even read of a cat who begged to have the roof of his mouth massaged! The side of the jaw between ear and chin is a definite yes: You may have noticed your cat forcefully rubbing everything within reach with the scent glands in her cheeks (marking). Expect intense purring.

EXPLORE NEW TERRITORY Think of a cat's ears the way humans think of their feet. We don't like it when they're tickled, and that's why foot doctors know to touch them firmly. Gently massage the back edge of your cat's ears between your thumbs and forefingers, using a circular, almost tugging motion at the tips. Some swear that this puts cats into a hypnotic state—but if your furry pal doesn't like it, don't force it! Keep returning to your pet's favorite spots between new territories. Stroking along the backs of the hind legs, if the cat tolerates it, triggers a reflex that looks as if the cat is doing the splits.

PLAY "THIS LITTLE PIGGY" Try massaging your cat's foot pads, tugging gently on her toes while she's relaxed and lying on her side. She likes it if she spreads her feet and extends her legs toward you, or, if lying on her back, she "pedals" an imaginary bicycle.

Clicker Training
Practical Clicking*

Get Off the Counter!

The method that trainers employ to replace undesirable behaviors is called *training an incompatible behavior*.

Your cat probably gets on the counter because she gets attention for it—even negative attention. Place a fairly high chair or stool near the counter. At first, click and treat the cat whenever she jumps to the chair. Clicking with your mouth is fine. She will soon realize that being on the counter gets her nothing, but jumping to the chair earns rewards. Sitting on the chair is incompatible with counter surfing. After a while, stop treating her each time. The behavior will only get stronger as she tries to get your attention in the way she's now conditioned. Give her food or affection every so often. This is called a *variable interval of reinforcement*, and is one of the most effective tools of operant conditioning.

In the event your little surfer gets up to mischief while you are out, you can use *aversives*. Cover the counter with foil and sprinkle it with water (cats don't like walking on foil). Line the edge of the counter with cans filled with just enough pennies to

198

Practical Clicking

make noise—not too heavy to be knocked off (don't test this in front of the cat). The foil and the loud noise of the penny cans will make that counter an unpleasant place to be. You should have to do this for only about a week. Combine this method with the chair solution above. Oh, and make sure you don't store your cat's food on or near the counter.

*Assumes your cat is clicker-wise.

Practical Clicking

Clipping Claws

Teach your cat the Gimme Five (page 113). Make sure he is doing it consistently. When he lays his paw in your hand, begin by very gently holding it for a fraction of a second longer. CT! Resist the urge the urge to squeeze, grab, or forcibly hold the cat's leg. Over a series of sessions, gradually move to lifting a toe for a second. Do not try to clip—just look at a claw, drop the paw, CT! Some cats take days or a couple of weeks to get to this point. Use baby steps and treats until finally you can zoom in and clip a tiny end off one claw without his fighting you. Jackpot your pet! Now things will get much easier, because he realizes that each clip means a treat. Eventually you will have a cat who presents his paw for a manicure, or at least will allow you to clip without a fight.

Carriers

This is a project for the cat and human with clicker experience. It will probably take three weeks of short daily sessions.

Your cat should know Touch well enough to come to the prop from across a room. Use a Sherpa Bag or similar cat-comfy carrier. Leave the carrier out for a few days. Play Magic Box

Practical Clicking

(page 134) with your cat. Use the prop you used to teach Touch to gradually lead your 'fraidy cat closer (click and treat) and finally into the carrier. Click and treat for putting even one paw into the carrier. You can even put treats just inside the door if it will get her head in there. Do not touch the cat. If she goes inside, do not close the door; click and toss in a treat. You might feed the cat her dinner there, once she gets used to going inside. Eventually you will find her in the carrier, waiting for a treat.

Once she's opting to stay inside the carrier regularly, try closing the door for a second, click and treat. The cat will pop right out at first, and you'll have to backtrack. Keep lengthening the time you close the door as she gets used to this activity. If she approves, let her sit for a short time with the carrier closed (poke treats in; if she's not too scared to eat, she's okay). Continue leaving the carrier out and giving rewards at random to strengthen the association with food. Lengthen the time with door closed at each session.

Follow the same baby steps for conditioning your cat to the car!

*Assumes your cat is clicker-wise.

To a
Cat

by
John Keats

Cat! who hast pass'd thy grand climacteric,
　　How many mice and rats hast in thy days
　　Destroy'd? How many tit-bits stolen? Gaze
With those bright languid segments green, and
　　prick
Those velvet ears—but prythee do not stick
　　Thy latent talons in me—and tell me all thy frays,
Of fish and mice, and rats and tender chick;
Nay, look not down, nor lick thy dainty wrists—
　　For all the wheezy asthma—and for all
Thy tail's tip is nick'd off—and though the fists
　　Of many a maid have given thee many a maul,
Still is thy fur as when the lists
　　In youth thou enter'dst on glass-bottled wall.

Sardine Sandies

Cats' ideas about what constitutes a cookie are very different from our own! If you have more than one cat, expect to find a convention of furry beggars underfoot as you prepare these. Choose whole sardines that have no salt added in processing (you can add your own).

$1/_3$ can sardines, drained, with $1/_2$ teaspoon oil reserved

200 IU vitamin E (from a capsule), as an antioxidant

$1/_3$ cup plain bread crumbs or cracker crumbs

1 egg, beaten

$1/_2$ teaspoon brewer's yeast

dash of salt

1. Preheat the oven to warm or its lowest setting.
2. In a small bowl, mash the sardines very well. Puncture the vitamin E capsule and drizzle it over the fish.
3. Add the remaining ingredients and mix well.
4. Drop tiny portions about the size of the tip of your little finger onto a cookie sheet generously greased with butter or shortening (cats don't have to worry about cholesterol). Do not form into balls; they don't bake well, and cats can't bite into them easily.
5. Dry in the oven for 40 minutes, turning once halfway through. Stored in an airtight container in the fridge, these keep for 4–5 days.

Makes 7–8 dozen.

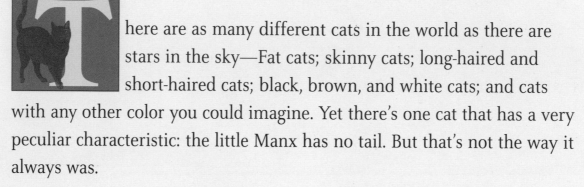

CAT TALES

There are as many different cats in the world as there are stars in the sky—Fat cats; skinny cats; long-haired and short-haired cats; black, brown, and white cats; and cats with any other color you could imagine. Yet there's one cat that has a very peculiar characteristic: the little Manx has no tail. But that's not the way it always was.

How the Manx Cat Lost His Tail

A Western European Tale

Long ago, back when Noah was first preparing for the Great Flood by building the Ark, the Manx cat had a beautiful, long tail that was the envy of all the other animals. And this is the story of how he lost it.

God told Noah that a flood was about to wash over the world, cleansing it of wickedness and sin, and that the only ones

206

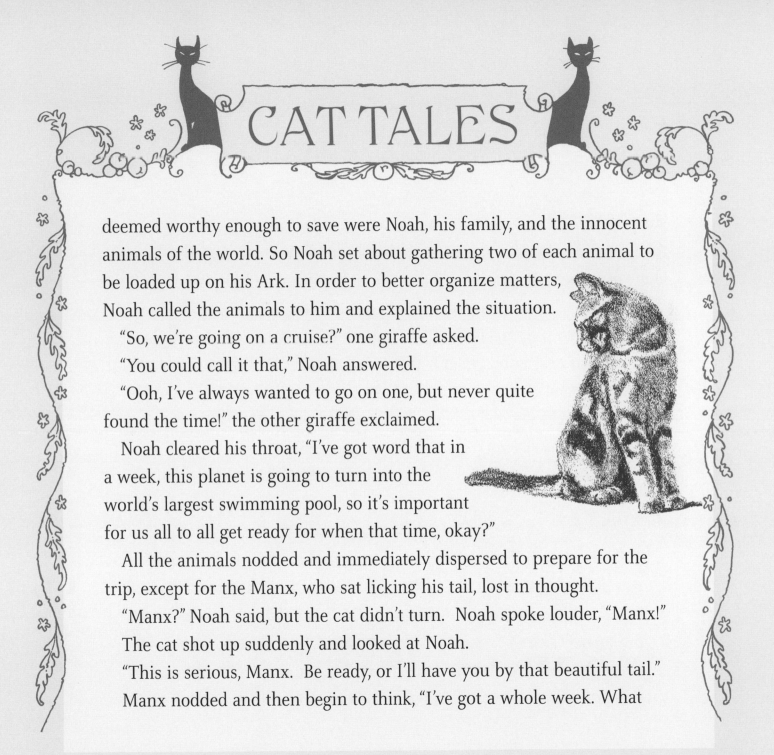

CAT TALES

deemed worthy enough to save were Noah, his family, and the innocent animals of the world. So Noah set about gathering two of each animal to be loaded up on his Ark. In order to better organize matters, Noah called the animals to him and explained the situation.

"So, we're going on a cruise?" one giraffe asked.

"You could call it that," Noah answered.

"Ooh, I've always wanted to go on one, but never quite found the time!" the other giraffe exclaimed.

Noah cleared his throat, "I've got word that in a week, this planet is going to turn into the world's largest swimming pool, so it's important for us all to all get ready for when that time, okay?"

All the animals nodded and immediately dispersed to prepare for the trip, except for the Manx, who sat licking his tail, lost in thought.

"Manx?" Noah said, but the cat didn't turn. Noah spoke louder, "Manx!" The cat shot up suddenly and looked at Noah.

"This is serious, Manx. Be ready, or I'll have you by that beautiful tail." Manx nodded and then begin to think, "I've got a whole week. What should I do with myself for a whole week? Wait a minute! Only a week, then the only mice I'll see for a while will be the two on the Ark. And I won't even be able to touch them!" This thought made him so miserable, that he began hunting as many mice as he could, as fast as he could.

The week quickly passed quickly, and on the last day, ominous storm clouds began rolling in. Noah had finished the Ark and was ready for his first passengers.

"Okay, let's get a move on now," he ordered the animals, as they began to file onto the Ark.

"You're sure we'll be safe on there?" one gazelle asked as he eyed the lions suspiciously.

"Absolutely," replied Noah, "Now step right up, biggest to smallest!"

While the rest of the animals were lining up to board the Ark, the Manx cat was still busy chasing mice. He stopped to notice the other animals waiting to get on the Ark and declared, "Oh, I have plenty of time before it's my turn!" Then he jumped at an unsuspecting rodent.

The hours went by, and fat drops of rain began to fall. Two of each animal were carefully noted and then led onto the ship. By the time they

CAT TALES

CAT TALES

were at the mid-sized armadillos, large pools of water were growing rapidly on the ground.

But the Manx cat continued to catch mice. "Aren't you coming?" asked the skunks, as they passed him by.

"Sure, sure," he said, barely looking up, "Just one more mouse. I'll be right there."

By the time Noah reached the end of the line, there was barely any dry land left to stand on and every animal had been loaded onto the Ark, except the Manx.

"Come on Manx!" Noah called. "We've got a schedule to keep here!"

"Just one more mouse!" the cat called back, "One more and I'll be there."

"We don't have time for this, Manx cat!" Noah answered. "It's now or never!"

But the Manx cat had just pounced upon a juicy morsel and was about to finish it off. Suddenly, the mouse slipped from the cat's grip and bolted.

"Oh bother," he declared, as he chased the scurrying mouse.

Now, luckily for the Manx cat, the mouse was heading directly for the Ark door, where at that very moment, they were closing up the ship. Quick as a wink, the mouse darted inside and directly behind him came the Manx cat!

But just as he had pounced on the little mouse inside, he let out an ear-splitting screech, "YOOOWWWW!!"

For you see, although most of the Manx cat was inside the Ark, its poor, beautiful tail had still not made it across the threshold, and before he knew what had happened, the door shut tight. The Manx cat was left with nothing but a sorry looking rump, while his long tail was left outside. He was so distraught that he let go of the little mouse, and wept and yowled over the fate of his poor tail.

The rest of the animals tried to console him, but Noah said, "Serves you right. Let that be a lesson to you! Never let pleasure get in the way of what needs to be done."

And to this day, the Manx cat is a very meek and modest creature. Perhaps because it remembers its luxurious tail lost so long ago.

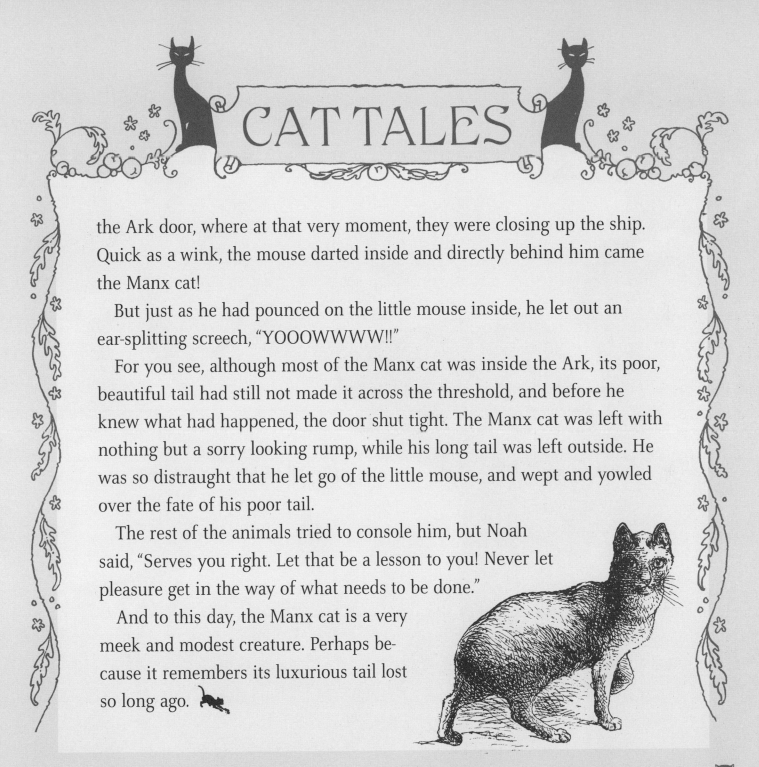

Stair Bounce

If you find the right big, light, soft fuzzy ball, cats will vote for the Stair Bounce as Best Cat Game, every time. Children, too, can be entertained by Kitty's upstairs-downstairs antics for hours. This game is great for "wearing out" mischeivous kittens who have a penchant for getting into everything. Cats find sheepskin-covered balls particularly irresistible.

> lightweight, medium- to large-size fleece or sheepskin-covered ball (around 6-inches maximum) from a pet supply store; a "step-wise" cat

1. Use a lightweight toy that rolls and bounces, and is soft enough for a cat to sink her teeth and claws into. Do not use a sparkle ball or other smooth, heavy ball that the cat can't grab. A sheepskin ball or large, soft foam ball is perfect. If it's catnip-impregnated, that's even better. Test the ball by rolling it to the cat. She may bite it and throw her legs around it while on her back, "gutting" it with her hind feet. This is what you want.

2. Lure her to the stairs. Start by dropping the ball gently from a few steps up, letting it roll down toward her for the "ambush."

3. Once she's on the stairs, go to the bottom and toss the ball up the stairs above the cat. She will learn to lie in wait for the ball to bounce over her. Cats often latch on to the ball, flopping down the stairs as they "kill" it and let off steam.

Shower Pong

This activity seems to be every cat's favorite, and it's especially good for a not uncommon behavioral problem: that unpleasant habit of peeing in the shower or bathtub. You've tried everything—cleaning and de-scenting, keeping plenty of clean litter boxes around—but Ms. Whiskers still thinks the shower is a giant litter box. This approach is called training an incompatible behavior, since cats will not normally pee where they play (or where they eat).

1. Open a package of Ping-Pong balls and start bouncing them around the shower or bath enclosure. If the noise doesn't draw feline fans, check your cats for a pulse! Lure them toward the bath-room with a ball.
2. Sit back and laugh. This activity is so much fun for cats, it's what's known as self-reinforcing. It doesn't require rewards, but you can sweeten the pot by giving treats to shy types for batting balls around.
3. Leave a couple of balls in the shower, and expect Pong to go on at any hour, once your cat gets the hang of it.
4. If your cat still has potty slipups, feed her in the tub exclusively for a few days. Animals will not toilet in an area they have learned to associate with food. If she does, suspect a bladder infection.

Sylvester's Health Biscuits

Just like ours, your cat's sensitive skin gets dried out by winter's indoor heat. But what if Kitty keeps turning up his nose at that terrific liquid coat supplement you are proffering him with? Keep that glossy coat in shape by hiding it inside this delicious biscuit.

$1/2$ can tuna in oil, drained, with 2–4 tablespoons oil reserved

$1/2$ cup whole wheat flour

$1/2$ cup nonfat powdered milk

1 tablespoon liquid coat supplement or cod liver oil

1 egg, beaten

1 small jar chicken baby food (without onion powder)

1. Preheat the oven to 350°F.
2. In a large bowl, mash the tuna; add the flour and powdered milk. Mix thoroughly.
3. Stir in the coat supplement or oil, egg, and baby food. Blend in enough of the reserved tuna oil to make the dough easier to handle.
4. Flour your hands well and form the dough into small, flattened biscuits. Place on a greased cookie sheet.
5. Bake for 10–12 minutes, flipping the biscuits halfway through. Refrigerate in a sealed container for up to a week.

Makes about 8 dozen biscuits.

Kitty Beach

This installation comes from a cat friend with a large loft, a roomy bathroom, and two dignified, aging cats. His pets appreciated it by taking extended holidays there. Using a camera placed on a tripod and equipped with a timer, he managed to photograph them in some very "undignified" sleeping positions.

Vacation Station

lamp, towel, water bowl, plastic palm tree from a hobby store or novelty shop (you can also find mini props like sunglasses and picnic baskets), sheet of poster board about 8" x 14", scissors, X-Acto knife, large stick-on letters

1. Set up a heat lamp in your bathroom or other nondrafty, out-of-the-way area a few feet above the floor. Use a clamp light with a ceramic socket and metal shade from the hardware store—you also can rig it to a tripod or use a floor lamp. If you don't have a heat lamp, a regular incandescent bulb will do.

2. Place a thick, fluffy beach towel underneath the lamp. Arrange it around the drinking bowl to make this look like a pool. Add the plastic palm tree and other props to your set.

3. Cut out a piece of poster board and score it lightly crosswise in the center. Fold in half so that it will stand up. Use the display lettering to make a funny sign that reads KITTY BEACH, CATATONIC ISLAND, NO SWIMMING WITHOUT LIFEGUARD ON DUTY, or other humorous statement.

Vacation Album

camera, tripod, timer (optional)

1. Take snapshots of "vacationing" felines every half hour or other interval. It's most convenient to prefocus your camera and set it up

Kitty Beach

on a tripod so that all you have to do is click the shutter every so often. For the ultimate vacation album, use a self-timing device (from a photo supply store) that will take shots at set intervals over a 24-hour period. You will catch cats washing, "sunbathing," sleeping together, and probably even tussling over the warmest spot.

2. Print out and paste snapshots in a photo album with captions about their "vacation," or store photos in a digital album on your computer. E-mail them to friends!

On the death of a favorite cat,
drowned in a tub of goldfishes.

Ode

by
Thomas
Gray

'Twas on a lofty vase's side,
Where China's gayest art had dyed
 The azure flowers that blow;
Demurest of the tabby kind,
The pensive Selima, reclined,
 Gazed on the lake below.

Her conscious tail her joy declared;
The fair round face, the snowy beard,
 The velvet of her paws,
Her coat, that with the tortoise vies,
Her ears of jet, and emerald eyes,
 She saw, and purred applause.

Still had she gazed; but 'midst the tide
Two angel forms were seen to glide,
 The genii of the stream:
Their scaly armor's Tyrian hue
Through richest purple to the view
 Betrayed a golden gleam.

The hapless nymph with wonder saw:
A whisker first and then a claw,

Animals play an important role in fiction, even if only as nameless fireside companions. A book without at least one pet is a cold piece of fiction indeed—even Shakespeare had his Grimalkin. In the ragingly popular Harry Potter series, Hermione acquires a cat named Crookshanks, while Fitch's pet, the terrible Mrs. Norris, patrols the halls of Hogwarts. Mystery writer Rita Mae Brown gets help from feline co-writer Sneaky Pie Brown. The classics give us such well-known cat characters as the Cheshire Cat (Alice's Adventures in Wonderland), Figaro (Disney's version of Pinocchio), Sher Khan (The Jungle Book), and Tigger (Winnie-the-Pooh). Stephen King brings back to life the cat Church in Pet Sematary, while Capri was companion to the multiple personalities of Sybil's protagonist. And what could be a more perfect

Literary Cats

name for a lioness than Elsa, of Born Free? Finally, we wonder how many cat lovers have named their beloved pets after Don Marquis's famous Mehitabel, who claims to be a reincarnation of Cleopatra. Some wonderful felines jump out at us from literature:

222

LADY JANE, from Dickens's *Bleak House* • **CHATTIE**, from Mary Augusta Ward's *Robert Elsmere* • **WOTAN**, from Henry Handel Richardson's *Maurice Guest* • **MOUMOUTTE BLANCHE** and **MOUMOUTTE CHINOISE**, from Pierre Loti • **PUFF, MURR,** and **BRISQUET**, from Balzac • **FRANCHETTE, SAHA,** and **KIKI-LA-DOUCETTE**, from Colette • **ALEXANDER FURBY**, from Ursula K. Le Guin's *Wonderful Alexander and the Catwings* • **BLOOMBERG**, from J. D. Salinger's *Franny & Zooey* • **BUSTOPHER JONES**, from T. S. Eliot's *Old Possum's Book of Practical Cats* • **CATASAUQUA**, from Mark Twain's *Letters from the Earth* • **CHILDEBRAND, ENJORAS, SÉRAPHITA, ZIZI,** and **EPONINE**, from Théophile Gautier's *La Ménagerie Intime* • **EATBUGS, GRIZRAZ HEARTEATER, POUNCEQUICK,** and **FIRSA ROOFSHADOW**, from Tad Williams's *Tailchaser's Song* • **ITTY**, from Hugh Lofting's Dr. Dolittle books • **MIDNIGHT LOUIE** and **MIDNIGHT LOUISE**, from Carole Nelson Douglas's books • **MITTENS, MOPPET, PERCY, SIMPKIN, SQUINTINA, TABITHA TWITCHIT,** and **MRS. RIBBY**, from Beatrix Potter's books • **NITCHEVO**, from Tennessee Williams's story "The Malediction" • **PICKLES**, from Esther Averill's *Pickles the Fire Cat* • **PIXEL**, from Robert Heinlein's books • **PLUTO**, from Edgar Allan Poe's "The Black Cat" • **RHUBARB**, from H. Allen Smith's *Rhubarb* • **SIR GREEN-EYES GRIMALKIN DE TABBY DE SLY**, from Laura E. Richards's "The Sad Story of the Dandy Cat" • **TATTOO** and **PINKLE PURR**, from A. A. Milne's poem "Pinkle Purr" • **WEBSTER**, from P. G. Wodehouse's "The Story of Webster" • **ZAPAQUILDA**, from Lope de Vega's *The Battle of the Cats*.

A cat's a cat and
that's that.

—AMERICAN FOLK SAYING